The One-Bowl BAKER

The *One-Bowl* BAKER

Easy,
UNFUSSY RECIPES
for Decadent Cakes, Brownies,
Cookies and Breads

STEPHANIE SIMMONS
founder of Blue Bowl Recipes

PAGE STREET
PUBLISHING CO.

PAGE STREET
PUBLISHING CO.

First published in 2022 by

Page Street Publishing Co.

27 Congress Street, Suite 105

Salem, MA 01970

Distributed by Macmillan, sales in Canada by The Canadian Manda Group.

26   25   24   23   22   1   2   3   4   5

ISBN-13: 978-1-64567-364-4

ISBN-10: 1-64567-364-2

Library of Congress Control Number: 2021930245

Cover and book design by Meg Baskis for Page Street Publishing Co.

Photography by Stephanie Simmons

Printed and bound in China

Dedication

To Grant, my biggest supporter, encourager and most-trusted taste tester

Contents

INTRODUCTION

I'm a firm believer that the recipes in this book are things that anyone can make—this isn't your finicky French patisserie type of baking. I don't have the patience for that. (If you do, kudos!)

On my blog, Blue Bowl Recipes, I try to focus on classic baking recipes while giving many of them my own approachable spin or a modern twist—and I've taken the same approach in this cookbook.

Instead of classic peanut butter cookies, we're making Peanut Butter and Jelly Thumbprint Cookies (page 24). A classic yellow cake with chocolate frosting gets an upgrade from malt powder to turn it into a Malted Vanilla Birthday Cake with Chocolate Frosting (page 82). Traditional wedding-cake flavored cupcakes are transformed into something new and exciting—Raspberry Almond Cupcakes (page 65)—by adding raspberry preserves to the center of the cupcakes and to the frosting.

You get the picture. These are recipes that don't require any wild or complicated techniques, and of course, they're all made in one bowl. I've done a little finagling here and there to keep the number of dishes down—using an already dirtied measuring cup for your egg wash or mixing wet ingredients together in a glass measuring cup instead of a separate bowl. No matter how simple a recipe, we still don't want to be left with a mountain of dishes in the sink at the end of it.

Some of these recipes do have a special finishing touch that might require a quick rinse of your batter bowl to make—like frosting on a cake or chocolate ganache on a tart. With these simple, beginner-friendly recipes, there's no need to be too fussy.

Even though I've added little shortcuts to these recipes and cut back on steps wherever I could, these are all recipes you can absolutely take to any event—potlucks, picnics, work gatherings, holiday parties—and get asked, "How did you make this? It's SO good! Can I have the recipe?"

And that's my goal: giving you recipes that you can bake no matter your level of baking experience, won't take you ages to make, won't leave you with a mountain of dirty bowls and will still trick people into thinking you're another Martha.

Make sure you take a moment to read my tips and tricks in the Baking Basics section (page 10). This will familiarize you with everything you need to know about my recipes and ensure the best baking success—especially if you consider yourself a novice in the kitchen.

I hope that this book has your new favorite thing to bake, and I hope that you share what you make with the people you love.

BAKING BASICS

Read the Recipe

I always recommend reading a recipe through before starting it to ensure you are aware of all chill or resting times and to double check that you have all the ingredients.

Preparing Baking Pans

You'll notice that on recipes that call for a baking dish to be lined with parchment paper, I say spray it with nonstick spray and line it. Spraying the pan with nonstick spray first helps the parchment paper adhere to the pan, so it's not jumping back out while there's nothing in the pan to hold it down. You can certainly skip this step; I just find it helpful.

All About Butter

The most common issue in the baking world (in my experience) is not softening your butter properly. Letting it sit at room temperature to soften on its own is the best method. I do not recommend microwaving it. This usually results in butter that's bordering on melted, instead of softened, which can affect your finished bakes (especially with cookies—this is usually why they spread too much in the oven!). When letting your butter come to room temperature naturally, don't let it sit out for too long. It shouldn't feel warm to the touch, and when you press your finger lightly into it, you shouldn't immediately make a huge indent. Your finger should make a small indent, without sinking into the butter. It shouldn't be shiny or feel greasy.

I use salted butter for everything, since I personally think it tastes much better than unsalted butter. However, if you want to use unsalted, feel free! I don't feel like you need to make any changes to the recipe to account for this.

Cutting Butter into Dry Ingredients

For any recipe that calls for butter to be cut into your dry ingredients, I recommend using a pastry cutter. It's easy and cuts down the time it takes to do this step. Some people recommend using a fork or your hands, but I personally prefer a pastry cutter and feel that it's a worthwhile tool to have around. You can find them at most stores that carry kitchen tools (Target, Walmart, etc.), and they're usually between $5.00 and $12.00. If you don't have or don't want to purchase a pastry cutter, you can use your (clean!) hands to rub the butter into the flour, breaking it up into pieces and making sure it's coated in flour—which is what a pastry cutter does.

Creaming Butter and Sugar

When you mix sugar into butter, cream it with your mixer on a higher speed for at least 30 seconds to a minute. You want the mixture to really come together. It shouldn't feel like light sandy crumbs; there should be a smidge of resistance from your mixer and the whole thing should feel like a more cohesive, moist mixture.

Measuring Flour

I know that everyone has a different way of measuring flour, but my preferred method is the scoop and level. Here's what that means: Dunk your measuring cup into your bag or jar of flour, and lift it out. Don't shake the measuring cup around or pack the flour. Simply take the flat edge of a butter knife and level off the flour that's piled over the edge of the measuring cup. This does yield a slightly higher amount of flour than if you did the spoon and level method, but I find that method to be slow and clunky. All my recipes are based off this easy way of measuring flour. So even if you're used to spooning and leveling, or if you're saying, "1 cup of flour is 120 grams, not 140," you should be aware that my recipes are measured this way and are based around 1 cup of flour weighing 140 grams. The one exception to this is with cake flour. I prefer to spoon and level it, and that's noted in the three recipes where I call for it.

Measuring Brown Sugar

Make sure you're packing the brown sugar in as you go. You should be packing the sugar down in between every few generous spoonfuls into your measuring cup. Make sure to level it off at the end, too, with the flat end of a butter knife.

Bake Time

Everyone's oven runs a little differently, and I suggest using an oven thermometer for the best baking accuracy. I also always start my bake time a few minutes under what the recipe says. So, if a recipe says to bake for 35 to 40 minutes, I'll probably start the timer at 30 or 35 minutes, especially if it's something I haven't made before. With things that have a shorter bake time, like cookies, I usually bake a single cookie first to make sure that the bake time is correct to my oven. This way, if your oven does run a bit hot, you can avoid overbaking and drying out a recipe. I always err on the side of starting with less time because you can always add a few more minutes . . . but you can't undo an overbaked dessert. I also prefer to bake just one thing in my oven at a time—one sheet of cookies, etc. This allows the oven to concentrate on just the one pan, giving you a more even bake. But if you are comfortable baking two pans at once, go for it! I do recommend rotating the top and bottom pan halfway through if you do this.

Modifying Recipes

Speaking of recipes turning out meh . . . I tested these recipes as they were written, and any modifications that I tested will appear in the notes for that recipe. Keep in mind that once you start making your own changes, I cannot guarantee that the recipe will still turn out. Some small changes will certainly not ruin a recipe, such as swapping strawberry jam for raspberry in the coffee cake or leaving out the coconut from the oatmeal cookie bars if coconut is not your thing. You might run into trouble if you choose to make larger changes, like changing one type of flour for another, or changing one type of sugar for another. If I call for all-purpose, use that unless otherwise stated in the recipe, and the same goes for sugar, etc. If you do want to experiment with different ingredient swaps, feel free! Just know that you may not end up with the best possible results.

COOKIES FOR ALL *Occasions*

Cookies—the quintessential dessert! Cookies have a place at almost every gathering or event you can think of. They just have a knack for bringing people together. You'll find them on bright platters at birthday parties and holiday gatherings, tucked into brown paper sacks for school lunches, in the cookie jar in the corner of your parents' kitchen and on the dessert tray at weddings and potlucks.

I've included cookies in this chapter that fit into all of these occasions! Make my Two Outrageously Huge Chocolate Chip Cookies (page 31) when you want a late-night snack but don't want to fuss with baking up two dozen cookies. Black Forest Cookies (page 16) and Peppermint Mocha Cookies (page 27) are no-chill, making them perfect for entertaining when you're in a pinch. There are fun flavors, like the Key Lime Slice-and-Bake Cookies with Key Lime Glaze (page 19) and the Peanut Butter and Jelly Thumbprint Cookies (page 24). And there are even modern twists on classic old-fashioned recipes, like my Brown Butter Oatmeal Raisin Cookies (page 20). And all of these can be made in one bowl! No need to whisk up your dry ingredients in a separate bowl first. I never, ever do that when I bake cookies, and I promise the results will still be phenomenal.

Whether you're digging into the warm, gooey Dulce de Leche Swirled Skillet Cookie (page 23) with spoons (forgoing plates entirely, which is the only way to properly enjoy it), mixing up the Insanely Fudgy Gluten-Free Chocolate Cookies (page 32) for the perfect movie-night treat or passing around a tray of Lemon Basil Cookies (page 35) at a potluck, I hope these cookies bring you joy!

BLACK FOREST *Cookies*

Hello, decadence! These cookies have milk and semisweet chocolate chunks, dried cherries and cherry kirsch all wrapped up in a soft and fudgy chocolate cookie. Drizzle chocolate ganache over the top, and fall head over heels for these simple-to-make cookies.

Yield: **16–18 COOKIES**

½ cup (1 stick or 113 g) salted butter, softened at room temperature

½ cup (120 g) packed brown sugar

½ cup (105 g) granulated or cane sugar

1 large egg

1½ tsp (8 ml) vanilla extract

1 tbsp (15 ml) cherry kirsch

1 cup (140 g) all-purpose flour

⅔ cup (65 g) cocoa powder

½ tsp baking soda

¼ tsp salt

3 oz (85 g) semisweet chocolate, chopped into chunks

3 oz (85 g) milk chocolate, chopped into chunks

¾ cup (126 g) chopped dried sweetened cherries

½ batch Chocolate Ganache (page 153)

PREP: Preheat the oven to 350°F (180°C). Line a baking sheet with parchment paper or a silicone baking mat.

MAKE THE COOKIES: In a large mixing bowl, cream the softened butter with an electric mixer. Add the brown sugar and granulated sugar and mix until well creamed, about 1 minute. Add the egg, vanilla and cherry kirsch, and mix until just combined. Add the flour, cocoa powder, baking soda and salt, and mix until just combined, scraping the sides of the bowl as needed. Mix in the semisweet chocolate, milk chocolate and the dried cherries.

BAKE: This dough has no chill time! Roll cookie dough into balls that are about 2 tablespoons (45 to 50 g) in size. Place the balls a few inches (8 cm) apart on the baking sheet. Bake for 8 minutes. The cookies will be a little puffy and have some cracks/wrinkles on top. They'll sink a bit and set up as they cool. Let them cool on the baking sheet for a few minutes, and then transfer them to a cooling rack to finish cooling.

MAKE THE CHOCOLATE GANACHE AND DECORATE: While the cookies cool, make half a batch of Chocolate Ganache (page 153). Let it cool for a few minutes, and then drizzle it over the cookies. You don't need to wait until they're completely cool to do this. Alternatively, you can just use melted chocolate.

SERVE AND STORE: Enjoy immediately, or let the chocolate set up first. Store leftover cookies in an airtight container at room temperature for 1 week or in the fridge for 2 weeks.

 Tip If you're doubling the recipe, don't double the salt.

KEY LIME SLICE-AND-BAKE *Cookies* WITH KEY LIME GLAZE

There's something so fun about making slice-and-bake cookies. There's a bit of an old-fashioned feel to these, but the flavor profile is anything but. These cookies practically melt in your mouth and are full of refreshing zingy key lime flavor, while requiring much less work than a key lime pie.

Yield: **24-26 COOKIES**

FOR THE COOKIES

¾ cup (1½ sticks or 170 g) salted butter, softened at room temperature

⅔ cup (160 g) packed brown sugar

1 large egg

1½ tsp (8 ml) vanilla extract

Zest of 1 large lime

2 tbsp (30 ml) key lime juice (add 1 extra tsp [15 ml] if using regular lime juice)

2 cups plus 1 tbsp (289 g) all-purpose flour

⅛ tsp cinnamon

¼ tsp salt

Coarse or raw sugar, for rolling

FOR THE GLAZE

1 batch Infinitely Adaptable Glaze (page 157)

2 tbsp plus ½ tsp (33 ml) lime juice (omit the extra ½ tsp if using key lime juice)

Lime zest

MAKE THE COOKIES: In a large mixing bowl, cream the softened butter with an electric mixer. Add the sugar and mix until well combined. Add the egg, vanilla, lime zest and lime juice and mix until just combined. Add the flour, cinnamon and salt and mix just until the last streaks of flour disappear into the dough.

Divide the dough into two equal sections. Shape into logs that are about 8 to 9 inches (20 to 23 cm) long and 2 to 3 inches (5 to 8 cm) wide. Pour your coarse or raw sugar onto a plate and roll each dough log through it to cover in the sugar. Wrap each log separately in plastic wrap. Place each log inside a drinking glass laid on its side so it is encapsulated inside the glass. This helps keep the cookies round while they chill. Chill in the freezer for 1 hour or in the fridge for at least 2 hours, or overnight.

Preheat the oven to 350°F (180°C). Line two baking sheets with parchment paper or a silicone baking mat.

Unwrap one of the dough logs. Move the other from the freezer to the fridge so it doesn't freeze solid on you. Slice the log into 12 to 14 even slices.

Place the cookies at least 2 inches (5 cm) apart on one prepared baking sheet. If the cookie dough softened quite a bit while you worked with it, pop the sheet back in the fridge to chill for 5 minutes before baking. Repeat all the steps with the remaining dough log.

BAKE: Bake one sheet of cookies at a time for 14 to 16 minutes. The edges will have a hint of golden brown. Let the cookies cool for a few minutes on the baking sheet, and then transfer them to a cooling rack to cool completely.

MAKE THE GLAZE: While the cookies are cooling, whisk together all the glaze ingredients along with the lime juice and a few pinches of lime zest.

SERVE AND STORE: When the cookies are cool, dunk them in the glaze, and enjoy! Store leftovers, once the glaze has set, in an airtight container at room temperature for 3 to 4 days.

BROWN BUTTER OATMEAL RAISIN *Cookies*

Growing up, my favorite cookie was oatmeal raisin—not the ever-popular chocolate chip. Gasp! I know, I know, I'm a strange one. But if you've had a really good oatmeal raisin cookie, I'm sure you understand just where I'm coming from. These are thick and soft, and the brown butter along with a hint of cinnamon and nutmeg lifts the flavor of these cookies to their rightful place alongside chocolate chip cookies.

Yield: **21 COOKIES**

1 cup (2 sticks or 226 g) salted butter

1 cup (240 g) packed brown sugar

½ cup (105 g) granulated sugar

2 large eggs

1 tsp vanilla extract

1½ cups (210 g) all-purpose flour

1 tsp baking soda

1½ tsp (4 g) cinnamon

½ tsp nutmeg

⅛ tsp cloves

½ tsp salt

3 cups (312 g) old-fashioned whole rolled oats

1 cup (145 g) raisins

BROWN THE BUTTER: In a nonstick pot or pan, melt the butter over medium heat. Turn the heat to medium-low, and continue cooking the butter, stirring constantly. The butter will get foamy and bubbly, and then turn a deep golden shade with a nutty, caramelly aroma. Once it reaches a deep golden color, (this will take about 5 to 6 minutes after the butter melts), remove it from the heat and pour it into a large mixing bowl. Pop this in the fridge, covered or uncovered, for 1 hour and 20 minutes, so the butter can reach the consistency it would be if you softened it at room temperature.

MAKE THE COOKIES: Once the brown butter has chilled, beat it with an electric mixer to cream it. Add the brown sugar and granulated sugar, and mix until well creamed with the butter, making sure all the little brown bits of the butter from the bottom of the bowl are incorporated. Add the eggs and vanilla and mix just until the eggs disappear into the batter. Add the flour, baking soda, cinnamon, nutmeg, cloves and salt, and mix until the last streaks of dry ingredients just disappear into the dough. Scrape the sides of the bowl. Add the oats and mix just to evenly distribute, and then do the same with the raisins.

Chill the cookie dough, covered, for 30 minutes in the fridge. While the cookie dough is chilling, prepare a few cookie sheets with parchment paper or silicone baking mats. Preheat the oven to 350°F (180°C). Note: These cookies do NOT hold up better the longer you chill them. Don't chill the dough overnight, or really for longer than 1 hour.

BAKE: Scoop the chilled cookie dough into balls that are about 3 tablespoons (60 g). Place them a few inches (8 cm) apart on the baking sheet. (I usually get six to eight on one sheet.) Bake for 10 minutes. The cookies will look a little underdone, but that's what we want. They'll set up as they cool. Keep the cookie dough in the fridge, covered, between baking batches. You can roll all the dough balls right away, and then pop them back in the mixing bowl, covered, to chill while you bake each pan. Let the cookies cool on the baking sheet for 5 to 10 minutes, and then transfer them to a cooling rack to finish cooling (or eat them right off the tray—my favorite move).

SERVE AND STORE: Enjoy while the cookies are warm out of the oven. Store cooled cookies in an airtight container at room temperature for 4 to 5 days.

DULCE DE LECHE SWIRLED
SKILLET *Cookie*

You know that glorious moment when you bite into a fresh-out-of-the-oven cookie, and it's warm and gooey in the center? Well, this is one HUGE cookie that has a HUGE gooey center for you to dive into! I highly recommend forgoing plates or slices entirely with this recipe, and going straight from pan to spoon to mouth.

Yield: 6–8 SERVINGS

1 cup (2 sticks or 226 g) salted butter, softened at room temperature

¾ cup (180 g) packed brown sugar

¾ cup (158 g) granulated sugar

1 tsp vanilla extract

2 large eggs

2⅔ cups (370 g) all-purpose flour

1 tsp baking soda

¼ tsp salt

¾ cup (230 g) dulce de leche

Flaky sea salt (optional; I love Maldon's brand)

PREP: Preheat the oven to 350°F (180°C). Spray a 10-inch (25-cm) oven-safe skillet with nonstick spray.

MAKE THE COOKIE: In a large mixing bowl, cream the butter with an electric mixer. Add the brown sugar and granulated sugar and mix until well combined and creamed with the butter. Add the vanilla and eggs, and mix until just combined. Add the flour, baking soda and salt, and mix until they just disappear into the dough, scraping the sides of the bowl as needed. Evenly spread the cookie dough into the prepared pan, and then spoon the dulce de leche into dollops on top. Use a butter knife to swirl it around.

BAKE: Bake for 28 to 32 minutes. Let the cookie set up for about 10 to 15 minutes once it's out of the oven.

SERVE AND STORE: Sprinkle flaky sea salt on top, if you're into that, and enjoy while it's warm from the oven. The more you let it cool, the more it will set up—but with a skillet cookie like this, you kind of have to eat it while it's warm and gooey. Store leftovers in an airtight container at room temperature for 2 to 3 days or in the fridge for up to 5 days. Gently reheat slices in the microwave to get a little of that gooeyness back.

Tip You can microwave the dulce de leche a bit first to make it easier to swirl in.

PEANUT BUTTER AND JELLY THUMBPRINT *Cookies*

One bite and these cookies will transport you back to your childhood and memories of eating sticky, gooey, perfect peanut butter and jelly sandwiches for lunch, along with a cold glass of milk. That's the flavor of these cookies—in a slightly more sophisticated looking package. I'm partial to raspberry preserves, but you can swap whatever flavor of jam you love most. Just be sure to keep the cold glass of milk in the mix.

Yield: 18 COOKIES

½ cup (1 stick or 113 g) salted butter, softened at room temperature

½ cup (130 g) creamy peanut butter

½ cup (105 g) granulated sugar, plus extra for rolling

½ cup (120 g) packed brown sugar

1 large egg

½ tsp vanilla extract

½ tsp baking powder

¼ tsp salt

1½ cups (210 g) all-purpose flour

1 (18-oz [510 g]) jar raspberry preserves

PREP: Preheat the oven to 350°F (180°C). Line two baking sheets with parchment paper.

MAKE THE COOKIES: In a large mixing bowl, cream the butter with an electric mixer. Add the peanut butter and mix until it's just combined with the butter. Add the granulated sugar and brown sugar, and mix until well creamed together with the butters. Scrape the sides of the bowl as needed. Add the egg and vanilla and mix until just combined. Add the baking powder, salt and flour and mix just until the last of the flour disappears into the dough.

Roll the dough into balls that are about 1½ tablespoons (38 to 40 g) in size. Add some granulated sugar into the measuring cup you used for the flour. Roll each ball in the sugar and place them on the prepared baking sheets. Use a fork to press the traditional crisscross design into the cookies. Use your thumb to press an indent into the center of each cookie over the crisscross, and add about 1 teaspoon of the preserves to each.

BAKE: Place the cookies on the prepared baking sheets about 2 inches (5 cm) apart. Place the second baking sheet in the fridge to chill while the first bakes. Bake each sheet for 8 to 9 minutes. Let the cookies cool a few minutes on the baking sheet, and then transfer to a cooling rack to cool completely.

SERVE AND STORE: Enjoy as soon as they're cool enough to eat. Store leftovers in an airtight container at room temperature for up to 5 days.

PEPPERMINT MOCHA *Cookies*

These are my ultimate Christmas cookie. They're no-chill (convenient!), come together in one bowl (naturally) and the recipe can be doubled—making it perfect for cookie exchanges and holiday parties. These cookies are soft and fudgy, and drizzling white chocolate or dark chocolate ganache on top, along with a flurry of crushed candy canes, takes them to another level entirely.

Yield: 16 COOKIES

½ cup (1 stick or 113 g) salted butter, softened at room temperature

½ cup (120 g) packed brown sugar

½ cup (105 g) granulated or cane sugar

1 large egg

1½ tsp (8 ml) vanilla extract

¾ tsp peppermint extract

1 cup (140 g) all-purpose flour

2 tsp (5 g) espresso powder

⅔ cup (65 g) cocoa powder

½ tsp baking soda

¼ tsp salt

1 batch Chocolate Ganache (page 153)

12 mini candy canes, crushed

PREP: Preheat the oven to 350°F (180°C). Line a baking sheet with parchment paper or a silicone baking mat.

MAKE THE DOUGH: In a large mixing bowl, cream the butter with an electric mixer. Add the brown sugar and granulated sugar and mix until well creamed, about 1 minute. Add the egg, vanilla and peppermint extracts and mix until just combined. Add the dry ingredients and mix until just combined, scraping the sides of the bowl as needed.

This dough has no chill time! Roll balls of cookie dough that are about 1½ tablespoons (35 to 40 g) in size. Place them a few inches (8 cm) apart on the baking sheet and bake for 8 minutes. The cookies will be a little puffy and have some cracks/wrinkles on top. They'll sink a bit and set up as they cool. Let them cool on the baking sheet for a few minutes, and then transfer them to a cooling rack to finish cooling.

While the cookies cool, make a batch of Chocolate Ganache (page 153). Crush the candy canes in a bag using the back of a metal measuring cup or a rolling pin. Drizzle on the ganache or dip the cookies in halfway to coat. Sprinkle the candy cane bits over the wet chocolate. Let them sit out for about 1 hour to let the chocolate set. It will be a miracle if you can wait that long before eating one! Store leftover cookies in an airtight container at room temperature for 1 week or in an airtight container in the fridge for 2 weeks.

> *Tip* You can skip the ganache and decorate the cookies with melted white, semisweet or dark chocolate if that's what you prefer.

> *Make-Ahead Tip*
> These cookies can be made 1 to 2 days ahead and stored in an airtight container until ready to decorate.

GRANDMA'S ALMOND CRESCENT *Cookies*

These are a staple at Christmastime in our house. The recipe comes from my Grandma Kay, and she passed it on to my mom, and Mom passed it to me. These are some of the simplest cookies you can make—and they're finished off with a simple-but-beautiful snow flurry of powdered sugar.

Yield: **32 COOKIES**

1 cup (2 sticks or 226 g) salted butter, softened at room temperature

2 cups (280 g) all-purpose flour

½ cup (105 g) granulated sugar

½ tsp almond extract

Powdered sugar, for decorating

PREP: Preheat the oven to 325°F (165°C). Line two (or more) baking sheets with parchment paper or silicone baking mats.

MAKE THE COOKIES: In a large mixing bowl, cream the butter with an electric mixer. Add the flour, sugar and almond extract, and mix until a crumbly dough forms. Then, get in there with clean hands and work into a cohesive dough.

Roll the dough into small balls that are about 1 scant tablespoon (20 g), and then roll them a bit on the counter to form a log. Then, shape each log into a crescent or "C" shape.

BAKE: Place the cookies on the prepared baking sheets. These don't spread a ton, and they're small, so you can fit more on a sheet. I can get about 12 to 15 on a sheet. Bake for 20 to 24 minutes, taking the cookies out before they start browning at the edges.

DUST WITH POWDERED SUGAR: Let the cookies cool for a few minutes on the baking sheets, and then transfer to a cooling rack to cool completely. Fill the mixing bowl with powdered sugar and dunk the cookies in it to coat completely.

SERVE AND STORE: Store the cookies in an airtight container at room temperature for up to 2 weeks.

TWO OUTRAGEOUSLY HUGE CHOCOLATE CHIP *Cookies*

This recipe is my dessert-mergency go-to! You know what I mean—you're craving something sweet but don't have a ton of ingredients on hand, and you don't really want to make two dozen cookies. This recipe is quick and simple and makes just two huge chocolate chip cookies: One for you and one for a friend, or, let's be real . . . two for you. You deserve it.

Yield: 2 LARGE COOKIES

¼ cup (½ stick or 57 g) salted butter, softened at room temperature

3 tbsp (45 g) granulated sugar

3 tbsp (42 g) packed brown sugar

2 tbsp (30 ml) of a beaten egg (this is about half an egg's worth)

½ tsp vanilla extract

⅔ cup (93 g) all-purpose flour

¼ tsp baking soda

Pinch salt

Generous ½ cup (110 g) semisweet chocolate chips

Flaky sea salt (optional; I love Maldon's brand)

MAKE THE COOKIES: In a medium mixing bowl, cream the butter with an electric mixer. Add the granulated sugar and brown sugar, and mix until creamed together. Add the egg and vanilla, and mix them in until they just disappear into the batter. Add the flour, baking soda and salt, and mix, scraping the sides of the bowl to get everything incorporated, until the last streaks of flour disappear into the dough. The dough will be very crumbly at first but will come together into a cohesive dough as you continue to mix it. Add the chocolate chips, and give it one last quick mix.

Cover the bowl with a clean kitchen towel and chill in the fridge for 30 minutes.

BAKE: Preheat the oven to 350°F (180°C). Line a baking sheet with parchment paper or a silicone baking mat.

Divide the dough in half and form into two large balls (about 6 ounces or 180 grams each). Place them on the baking sheet. Flatten the dough balls down a bit with your hands. Bake for 16 to 18 minutes, or until the cookies have a bit of golden brown around the edges. They'll also look pretty set on top. Let the cookies cool on the baking sheet for 5 to 10 minutes, and then dig in while they're warm with a glass of cold milk. Sprinkle on some flaky sea salt to take these to another level of perfection.

> *Tip* You can make the dough, shape it into two balls and freeze them. Bake at the same temperature, straight from the freezer, for 16 to 19 minutes.

INSANELY FUDGY GLUTEN-FREE CHOCOLATE *Cookies*

If you read "gluten-free" and got ready to make a quick dash away from this recipe, wait! I promise that you'd never in a million years guess that these were gluten-free if I hadn't told you. They're ridiculously fudgy, rich and full of chocolate chunks! I'd choose these over many gluten-full cookies.

Yield: **22 COOKIES**

4 oz (113 g) bittersweet chocolate, chopped (use a good quality baking bar, like Ghirardelli or Baker's)

2 cups (350 g) semisweet chocolate chips

6 tbsp (85 g) salted butter

3 large eggs

½ cup plus 1 tbsp (120 g) granulated sugar

1½ tsp (8 ml) vanilla extract

½ cup plus 2 tbsp (66 g) almond flour

2 tbsp (10 g) cocoa powder

¼ tsp baking soda

¼ tsp salt

6 oz (170 g) milk, semisweet or dark chocolate, chopped (you can use a mix of all three [my preference] or even use chocolate chips)

Flaky sea salt (optional; I love Maldon's brand)

MAKE THE COOKIES: Add the bittersweet chocolate, semisweet chocolate and butter to a large microwave-safe bowl, and microwave in 30-second intervals, stirring between each, until fully melted and smooth. The mixture will be super thick. Add the eggs and sugar, and with an electric mixer on high speed, beat for 4 minutes. Add the vanilla and give it a quick mix. Add the flour, cocoa, baking soda and salt, and mix until just combined. Mix in the chopped chocolate or chocolate chips. The mixture will be quite thick and might not seem quite like cookie dough. Don't worry, that's normal.

Cover the dough with a kitchen towel or plastic wrap and chill in the freezer for 30 minutes or in the fridge for 1 hour or up to overnight.

BAKE: Preheat the oven to 325°F (165°C). Line two baking sheets with parchment paper or silicone baking mats.

Scoop the cookie dough into balls about the size of 1½ tablespoons (50 g). Use a spoon to form these balls since the dough is too thick for a cookie scoop.

Place the dough balls 2 inches (5 cm) apart on the baking sheets (I did about six to seven cookies per sheet). Bake for 10 minutes if you chilled the minimum amount of time, or 11 minutes if you chilled longer than that. They will look underdone when you pull them out of the oven—that's normal. They'll set up more as they cool.

Let the cookies cool on the baking sheets for about 10 minutes, and then transfer them to a cooling rack to cool completely (or dig in while they're still warm—my preference!). Sprinkle the flaky salt over the cookies if you wish, and enjoy with a cold glass of milk.

SERVE AND STORE: Store leftovers in an airtight container at room temperature for about 1 week. I like popping a leftover cookie in the microwave for about 6 to 8 seconds to get it warm and gooey again.

LEMON BASIL *Cookies*

This is a recipe my mom has been making for years. We always have them in the summer and even freeze a batch of dough so we can add these to holiday cookie plates. These cookies are flavored with lemon basil, chopped pistachios and lemon, and it's just such a wonderfully light and unique flavor combination. Even picky eaters will love these—I've tested it.

Yield: 20-22 COOKIES

¾ cup (1½ sticks or 170 g) salted butter, softened at room temperature

¾ cup plus 3 tbsp (198 g) granulated sugar, divided

1 egg

Zest of 1 large lemon, about 1 tbsp (6 g)

1 tbsp (15 ml) fresh lemon juice

⅓ cup (15 g) chopped lemon basil (use regular basil if you can't find lemon basil)

⅓ cup (40 g) shelled and chopped pistachios, divided

2 cups (280 g) all-purpose flour

½ tsp baking soda

¼ tsp salt

MAKE THE COOKIES: In a large mixing bowl, cream the softened butter with an electric mixer. Add ¾ cup (158 g) of the sugar and mix until well creamed with the butter. Add the egg, mixing until just combined. Add the lemon zest, lemon juice, basil and 3 tablespoons (24 g) of the chopped pistachios, and mix until just combined. Add the flour, baking soda and salt, and mix until the dough comes together. It will be pretty crumbly at first, but it will come together.

Gather the dough into a ball and flatten slightly into a 1-inch (2.5-cm)-thick disk. Wrap in plastic wrap and chill in the fridge for 1 hour.

While the dough is chilling, preheat the oven to 350°F (180°C). Line a baking sheet with parchment paper or a silicone baking mat. Mix the remaining pistachios and the remaining sugar in a used measuring cup.

BAKE: Break off pieces of the chilled dough and shape into balls about 1½ tablespoons (30 to 35 g) each. Roll each ball in the sugar and pistachio mixture and place on the baking sheet, leaving about 2 inches (5 cm) between each cookie. (I can fit about eight on a baking sheet.) Bake for 10 to 12 minutes. Let cool a few minutes on the baking sheet before moving them to a cooling rack.

SERVE AND STORE: Enjoy these cookies as soon as they've cooled a bit. Once cooled, store in an airtight container at room temperature for 5 to 6 days.

Make-Ahead Tip The cookie dough can be made and refrigerated for 1 day before baking. The dough disk can also be frozen for up to 2 months. Move it to the fridge the day before you plan to bake the cookies so it can thaw.

BROWN SUGAR, CHOCOLATE CHUNK AND PECAN *Cookies*

These soft cookies come together in no time—and they're full of flavor! We've got crunch from the pecans; the rich, deep flavor of brown sugar; and of course, plenty of chocolate. Take these right over the top with a sprinkle of flaky sea salt . . . while they're still warm, of course.

Yield: **28-30 COOKIES**

1 cup (2 sticks, 16 tbsp or 226 g) salted butter, softened at room temperature

1 cup (240 g) packed brown sugar

½ cup (105 g) granulated sugar

2 tsp (10 ml) vanilla extract

2 large eggs

2⅔ cups (370 g) all-purpose flour

1 tsp baking soda

½ tsp salt

1 cup (116 g) roughly chopped pecans

10 oz (283 g) semisweet chocolate, chopped into chunks, plus extra for pressing in where needed

Flaky sea salt (I love Maldon's brand)

MAKE THE COOKIE DOUGH: In a large mixing bowl, cream the butter with an electric mixer. Add the brown sugar and granulated sugar, and mix until well combined and creamed with the butter. Add the vanilla and eggs, and mix until just combined. Add the flour, baking soda and salt, and mix until they just disappear into the dough, scraping the sides of the bowl as needed. Mix in the pecans and chocolate.

CHILL: Chill the cookie dough, covered with a clean kitchen towel, in the fridge for 30 minutes. Preheat the oven to 350°F (180°C).

BAKE: Scoop the dough into balls that are about 2 tablespoons (45 g) in size. Press any extra chocolate chunks into the dough balls in places where you want more chocolate! Bake for 9 minutes. The cookies will look a tad underdone but will set up as they cool. Let the cookies cool on a baking sheet for a few minutes, and then transfer to a cooling rack to cool completely.

SERVE AND STORE: Enjoy while warm with a sprinkle of flaky sea salt and a glass of cold milk! Store cooled cookies in an airtight container at room temperature for 4 to 5 days.

BLONDIES, BROWNIES *and* BARS

I am a brownie convert. Yes, you read that right. Growing up, I disliked brownies. Gasp! How is that possible? I don't think I had a decent brownie until I started baking on my own in college. My mom was more of a cookie baker than a brownie baker, so my main exposure to brownies were those dry and unexciting powdered sugar–dusted, store-bought squares that show up at your middle school class parties.

Luckily, these homemade brownies, blondies and bar cookies are anything but dry and boring; they're rich, fudgy and deeply flavored. And the flavor possibilities are endless. These are just about my favorite types of treats to bake because they're quick to throw together and can be cut into any size you please to stretch or shrink the yield. (I call that baker's prerogative, hah!) Plop the batter in one pan, throw it in the oven and bake.

From Nutella-Swirled Brownies (page 40) and Gooey S'mores Brownies with Toasted Marshmallows (page 44) to Funfetti Blondies with White Chocolate Ganache (page 52) and Cinnamon Streusel Apple Butter Bars (page 47), I turn to this category of dessert again and again for parties, picnics, potlucks and everything in between.

NUTELLA-SWIRLED *Brownies*

If you love rich, fudgy brownies with that paper-thin crackly top, and if you also happen to love Nutella, then you are about to develop a SERIOUS obsession with these brownies. They're not only one of the easiest desserts I know how to make, but also one of the most crowd pleasing. This is a blue ribbon–worthy dessert.

Yield: **12–24 BROWNIES**

1 cup (2 sticks or 226 g) salted butter

1½ cups (315 g) granulated sugar

½ cup (120 g) packed brown sugar

4 large eggs

1½ tsp (8 ml) vanilla extract

1 cup (140 g) all-purpose flour

⅔ cup (65 g) cocoa powder

½ tsp salt

⅛ tsp espresso powder

¾ cup plus ½ cup (386 g) Nutella, divided

PREP: Preheat the oven to 350°F (180°C). Spray a 9 x 13-inch (23 x 33-cm) pan with nonstick spray and/or line it with parchment paper.

MAKE THE BROWNIES: Melt the butter in a large mixing bowl in the microwave. Whisk in the granulated sugar and brown sugar. Whisk in the eggs and vanilla, and continue whisking for 1 minute. This helps develop that crackly layer on top of the brownies. Stir in the flour, cocoa powder, salt and espresso powder, scraping the edges of the bowl as needed to get everything mixed in. Stir in ¾ cup (226 g) of the Nutella. Pour the batter into your prepared pan and spread it out evenly. Plop the remaining ½ cup (160 g) of Nutella on top of the brownie batter in little blobs. Drag a butter knife through the Nutella blobs in all directions to create swirls.

BAKE: Bake the brownies for 34 to 38 minutes. The brownies will look just set, and a toothpick inserted into the center will come out with a very thin coating of moist fudgy batter.

SERVE AND STORE: Let the brownies cool for a couple of hours before slicing. I normally say to wait until they're completely cooled, but these are best when they're still pretty fresh from the oven. Store leftovers (hah!) in an airtight container at room temperature for 3 to 4 days or in the fridge for 5 to 6 days.

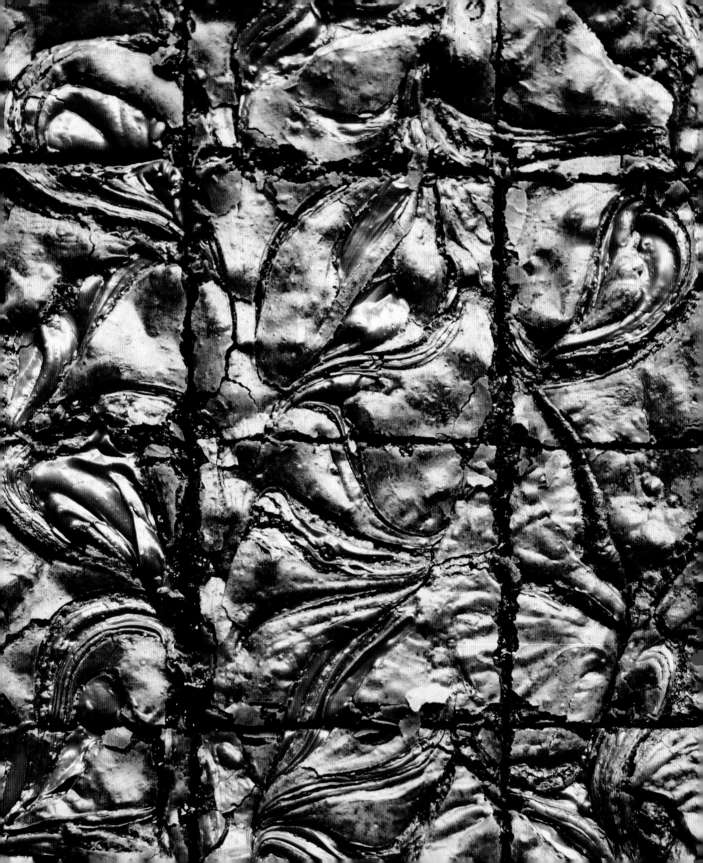

SNICKERDOODLE *Blondies*

This is the first recipe I tested for this book, and I think if I could only make one bar cookie for the rest of my life, it would be this one. Snickerdoodle Blondies taste just like soft-baked snickerdoodle cookies, and they practically melt in your mouth. It's the ultimate nostalgic, comfort-food dessert, and these are best served warm from the oven. So don't wait! You can be biting into one of these magical bars in less than an hour, and you'll be done doing the dishes long before these come out of the oven.

Yield: 12–24 SQUARES

FOR THE BLONDIES

1¼ cups (2½ sticks or 283 g) salted butter

1½ cups (315 g) granulated sugar

1 large egg

1 egg yolk

1½ tsp (8 ml) vanilla extract

2⅔ cups (370 g) all-purpose flour

1 tsp baking soda

¼ tsp salt

2 tsp (5 g) cream of tartar

1½ tsp (4 g) cinnamon

¼ tsp nutmeg

Pinch of ground cloves

FOR THE TOPPING

¼ cup (53 g) granulated sugar

1 tbsp (8 g) cinnamon

1 batch Infinitely Adaptable Glaze (page 157)

PREP: Preheat the oven to 350°F (180°C). Spray a 9 x 13-inch (23 x 33-cm) pan with nonstick spray and/or line it with parchment paper.

MAKE THE BLONDIES: Melt the butter in a large mixing bowl in the microwave. Whisk in the sugar. Add the egg, egg yolk and vanilla, and whisk until well combined. Add the flour, baking soda, salt, cream of tartar, cinnamon, nutmeg and cloves, and stir or whisk until well combined. Evenly spread the batter into the prepared pan.

MAKE THE TOPPING: Mix the sugar and cinnamon together in a dirtied measuring cup. Sprinkle this evenly over the top of the bars.

BAKE: Bake for 24 minutes. The center will seem a bit soft and not quite set, and the edges will be raised a bit and will appear set. A toothpick inserted into the center will come out clean or with a few moist crumbs. Top with 1 batch of my Infinitely Adaptable Glaze (page 157).

SERVE AND STORE: These are amazing while they're warm (I usually dive in after they sit for about 30 minutes), but they won't hold the neatest squares. To cut neat squares, let the bars cool for about 3 hours. Store leftovers, tightly covered, at room temperature for up to 4 days.

GOOEY S'MORES *Brownies* WITH TOASTED MARSHMALLOWS

These are the ultimate summertime treat! A thick layer of gooey, fudgy brownies sits atop a layer of graham crackers, and it's all nestled under a thick layer of melty chocolate and toasted-to-perfection marshmallows. Actually, scratch "ultimate summertime treat" and let's make these all year 'round.

Yield: **12-24 BROWNIES**

8 whole graham crackers

1½ cups (3 sticks or 339 g) salted butter

2½ cups (525 g) granulated sugar

½ cup (120 g) packed brown sugar

6 large eggs (No, that's not a typo, you do need 6 eggs!)

¼ tsp salt

1 tsp vanilla extract

1½ cups (210 g) all-purpose flour

1 cup (100 g) cocoa powder

12 caramel-filled chocolate squares (like Ghirardelli or something similar)

½ cup (100 g) milk chocolate chips

1 (16-oz [454-g]) bag mini marshmallows

PREP: Preheat the oven to 350°F (180°C). Spray a 9 x 13–inch (23 x 33–cm) baking dish with nonstick spray and/or line it with parchment paper. Place the whole graham crackers in the bottom of the baking dish in a flat layer, breaking pieces off as needed to fit the crackers in.

MAKE THE BROWNIES: Melt the butter in a large mixing bowl in the microwave. Whisk in the granulated sugar and brown sugar. Whisk in the eggs, 2 at a time, and then add the salt and vanilla and mix. Add the flour and cocoa powder, and stir until you have a smooth chocolate batter. Scrape the sides and bottom of the bowl with a spatula to make sure all the ingredients are incorporated.

BAKE: Pour the batter over the graham crackers. Bake for 43 to 47 minutes, or until a toothpick inserted in the edges of the brownies comes out clean and has some moist/gooey crumbs on it when inserted in the center of the brownies. Let the brownies cool for at least 3 hours or overnight before finishing them off with the marshmallow topping. If cooling overnight, let them cool a few hours at room temperature, and then cover them with foil until ready to finish.

When you're ready to serve the brownies, add the chocolate squares, chocolate chips and mini marshmallows (I never measure the marshmallows, I just cover the brownies in a generous layer) to the top of the brownies. Place the brownies under the broiler in the oven for 1 to 3 minutes to toast the marshmallows and melt the chocolate. Keep a close eye on the brownies so you don't burn the marshmallows.

SERVE AND STORE: Enjoy warm with a glass of cold milk. Cover leftover brownies tightly and store at room temperature for up to 3 days or in the fridge in an airtight container for up to 1 week. Re-warm in the microwave or oven if desired. (I'm a big fan of that.)

Tips *You can use both the milk chocolate chips and/or the chocolate caramel squares. If just using the milk chocolate chips, use 1 cup (200 g) and add more from there as desired.*

I don't recommend using large marshmallows in this recipe.

CINNAMON STREUSEL APPLE BUTTER *Bars*

These are some of the most popular bars I've ever made! They're made with one simple buttery crumble that does double duty as the base and topping for these treats. Spread apple butter between the two layers for an incredible—in taste and ease—dessert.

Yield: 9–12 BARS

¾ cup (1½ sticks or 170 g) salted butter

1½ cups (210 g) all-purpose flour

1 cup (98 g) old-fashioned whole rolled oats

1 cup (240 g) packed brown sugar

¾ tsp baking soda

½ tsp salt

1 tsp cinnamon

⅛ tsp nutmeg

1¼ cups (330 g) apple butter

PREP: Preheat the oven to 350°F (180°C). Spray a 9 x 9–inch (23 x 23–cm) pan with nonstick spray and/or line it with parchment paper.

MAKE THE BARS: Melt the butter in a large mixing bowl in the microwave. Whisk in the flour, oats, brown sugar, baking soda, salt, cinnamon and nutmeg, and stir together until well combined. You should have a crumbly mixture. Reserve 1 cup (210 g) of the mixture for the top of the bars. Press the rest into the bottom of your prepared pan.

BAKE: Bake for 10 minutes. Remove the pan from the oven and evenly spread the apple butter over the baked crust. Sprinkle the reserved crumble topping over the apple butter. Bake for 26 minutes, or until the topping looks cooked and lightly browned.

SERVE AND STORE: If you want nice neat squares, let the bars cool completely before slicing. If not, dig in while they're still warm. Store leftover bars in an airtight container at room temperature for 3 to 4 days or in the fridge for 5 to 6 days.

RASPBERRY WHITE CHOCOLATE CHEESECAKE *Bars*

Whoever said homemade cheesecake was complicated was wrong! These delightful bars are made using only eight simple ingredients—and I'm willing to bet you already have most of them in your kitchen. These cheesecake bars are light, creamy and swirled with delicious raspberry-flavored batter. Better make two batches of these because you won't want to share.

Yield: 9 SQUARES

FOR THE CRUST

5 tbsp (71 g) salted butter

1 cup (100 g) graham cracker crumbs

2 tbsp (26 g) granulated sugar

FOR THE FILLING

4 oz (113 g) white chocolate, finely chopped (use a good-quality baking bar, like Baker's or Ghirardelli)

12 oz (340 g) full-fat cream cheese, at room temperature

½ cup (105 g) granulated sugar

4 large eggs, at room temperature

1 tsp vanilla extract

¾ cup (240 g) raspberry preserves

PREP: Preheat the oven to 350°F (180°C). Spray a 9 x 9-inch (23 x 23-cm) pan with nonstick spray and/or line it with parchment paper.

MAKE THE CRUST: Melt the butter in a large mixing bowl in the microwave. Add the graham cracker crumbs and sugar, and stir well. Scrape the bowl well to get all the crumbs out and press this mixture into the bottom of your prepared pan. Bake for 8 minutes. Set aside to cool for at least 10 minutes while you make the filling.

MAKE THE FILLING: If there are any crumbs remaining in the bowl, give it a quick wipe with a clean kitchen towel. Add the chopped white chocolate to the same mixing bowl. Melt the chopped white chocolate in 15-second intervals in the microwave, stirring between each interval until it is completely melted and smooth. Add the cream cheese to the same bowl and mix until well creamed with the white chocolate. Add the sugar and mix until just combined. Add 2 of the eggs, and mix until just incorporated. Add the remaining eggs and vanilla and mix again until just incorporated. The batter will be mostly smooth, but you may see a few small flecks of cream cheese.

Scoop 1 cup of batter out of the mixing bowl and reserve in the measuring cup for later, and pour the rest into the prepared crust.

Add the reserved cup of batter back into the mixing bowl, and stir in the raspberry preserves. Spoon this over the top of the batter in the pan, and create swirls with a butter knife.

BAKE: Bake for 41 to 44 minutes. There should be only a slight jiggle in the center when you move the pan, and a toothpick inserted into the center will have a tiny bit of thick, moist batter.

SERVE AND STORE: Let the bars cool completely at room temperature, and then chill in the fridge, covered, for at least 3 hours or overnight before cutting and serving. Store leftovers in an airtight container in the fridge for 4 to 6 days.

PEANUT BUTTER CUP AND MILK CHOCOLATE–STUFFED *Blondies*

We all know peanut butter and chocolate are a match made in baker's heaven—and these blondies are stuffed full of both. It's like your favorite peanut butter cookies burst from their cocoon and came flying out as a milk-chocolate-studded peanut butter cup butterfly. Er, except the butterfly is actually these blondies. You get the picture—now get baking!

Yield: 9–18 SQUARES

1 cup (2 sticks or 226 g) salted butter

1 cup plus 2 tbsp (266 g) packed brown sugar

2 tbsp (26 g) granulated sugar

2 large eggs

2 tsp (10 ml) vanilla extract

1¾ cups (245 g) all-purpose flour

1 tsp baking powder

1 tsp baking soda

¼ tsp salt

¼ cup (68 g) creamy peanut butter

6 oz (170 g) milk chocolate, chopped into large chunks

18 small peanut butter cups (about 1½ cups [205 g]), halved or quartered (I like the Trader Joe's Dark Chocolate ones)

PREP: Preheat the oven to 350°F (180°C). Spray a 9 x 9–inch (23 x 23–cm) pan with nonstick spray and/or line it with parchment paper.

MAKE THE BLONDIES: Melt the butter in a large mixing bowl in the microwave. Whisk in the brown sugar and granulated sugar until completely mixed. Whisk in the eggs and vanilla until they're well mixed. Add the flour, baking powder, baking soda and salt, and stir until completely mixed, scraping the sides and bottom of the bowl to make sure everything gets mixed in.

Stir in the peanut butter. Reserve a handful of milk chocolate chunks and peanut butter cups, and stir the rest into the batter. Spread the batter evenly into the prepared pan. Sprinkle the reserved candies on top. Don't press them into the batter or they'll just get swallowed up while the blondies bake.

BAKE: Bake for 33 minutes, or until a toothpick inserted into the center has very few moist crumbs on it. It should be clean when inserted into the outside edge of the blondies.

SERVE AND STORE: Let the bars cool completely in order to cut into neat squares, or dig in sooner if you want to enjoy these while they're warm! Store at room temperature or in the fridge in an airtight container for up to 5 days. (If it's really hot in your place, like it is in ours—no central air conditioning—I definitely recommend keeping these in the fridge or they'll get pretty soft sitting out. I like to let them set at room temperature for a bit before eating, though.)

FUNFETTI *Blondies* WITH WHITE CHOCOLATE GANACHE

These blondies are like a birthday celebration in a pan! They've got that classic Funfetti flavor and plenty of colorful sprinkles to brighten up any occasion. Finish them off with a drizzle of White Chocolate Ganache (page 153) to take these to a whole new level.

Yield: 12-24 SQUARES

1 cup (2 sticks or 226 g) salted butter, softened at room temperature

2 cups (480 g) packed brown sugar

3 tbsp (40 g) granulated sugar

1 tbsp (15 ml) vanilla extract

3 large eggs

1 egg yolk

2⅓ cups (326 g) all-purpose flour

¼ tsp salt

1¼ tsp (6 g) baking powder

1¼ cups (228 g) sprinkles

½ batch White Chocolate Ganache (page 153)

PREP: Preheat the oven to 350°F (180°C). Spray a 9 x 13-inch (23 x 33-cm) pan with nonstick spray and/or line it with parchment paper.

MAKE THE BLONDIES: In a large mixing bowl, cream the butter with an electric mixer. Add the brown sugar and granulated sugar, and mix for about 1 minute, or until well creamed together and fluffy. Add the vanilla, eggs and egg yolk and mix until just combined. Add the flour, salt and baking powder, and mix again until just combined, scraping the sides of the bowl as needed. Reserve a handful or two of sprinkles for the top of the bars, and mix the rest into the batter. Spread the batter evenly into the prepared pan and sprinkle the extra handful of sprinkles on top.

BAKE: Bake for 33 to 36 minutes. The bars will be golden brown, and a toothpick inserted into the outside edges will be clean and have a bit of thick, moist battery crumbs when inserted into the center. The bars will jiggle a bit, too, when you move the pan. Never fear—they are baked. Blondies are meant to be a bit gooey, and they'll set up as they cool.

SERVE AND STORE: Drizzle the White Chocolate Ganache (page 153) over the blondies and dig in. You can enjoy these while they're still warm, but the longer you let them rest, the more they'll set up, allowing you to cut them into neat squares. Store leftovers in an airtight container at room temperature for 4 to 5 days.

S'MORES *Rice Krispie Treats*

A mashup of s'mores and rice krispie treats takes plain-Jane rice krispie treats to a whole new level. It's the perfect marriage of your favorite childhood and summertime treats. These chocolate squares are bursting with chocolate cereal and melty marshmallows, and they're topped with plenty of chocolate chips, more marshmallows and a dusting of graham cracker pieces. Don't skip the extra chocolate on top, either.

Yield: 9–18 SQUARES

¾ cup (1½ sticks or 170 g) salted butter

1 (16-oz [454-g]) bag mini marshmallows, divided

4½ cups (140 g) rice krispie cereal

1 tsp vanilla extract

¼ cup (50 g) semisweet chocolate chips

½ cup (35 g) graham cracker pieces (crumbs and small pieces), plus 1 whole cracker for topping

1 (4.4 oz [124 g]) milk chocolate candy bar, such as Hershey's

PREP: Spray an 8 x 8-inch (20 x 20-cm) pan with nonstick spray and/or line it with parchment paper. Measure all your ingredients before you begin so you don't leave the melted marshmallows unattended while you're grabbing ingredients later.

MAKE THE RICE KRISPIE TREATS: In a large nonstick pot or Dutch oven, melt the butter over medium heat. Reduce the heat to medium-low, and stir in 4½ cups (243 g) of the marshmallows. Keep stirring until you can no longer see the outline of any individual marshmallows. It should look like a cohesive puddle of buttery mallows. Stir in the cereal, vanilla, chocolate chips, graham cracker pieces and 1 cup (54 g) of the mini marshmallows.

Press the mixture evenly into the prepared pan. Break up the chocolate bar and scatter the pieces on top along with the remaining marshmallows. Crush the whole graham cracker into a mix of crumbs and small pieces, and sprinkle this over the top of the rice krispie treats.

SERVE AND STORE: Let the bars set for a few hours at room temperature before cutting. Store leftovers in an airtight container at room temperature for up to 3 days.

Tip *This recipe works well with vegan butter, vegan marshmallows and dairy-free chocolate. You can also use gluten-free graham crackers to keep the whole thing gluten-free and vegan.*

APRICOT, COCONUT AND WHITE CHOCOLATE OATMEAL COOKIE *Bars*

I love oatmeal raisin cookies—and I love riffing on that classic with unexpected flavors. These bars are just that! We're leaving behind the raisins in favor of a modern combination of dried apricots, coconut flakes and white chocolate chips. These bars are incredibly easy to make, and you can even drizzle them with White Chocolate Ganache (page 153) for an extra-fancy touch.

Yield: 12–24 BARS

½ cup (1 stick or 113 g) plus 2 tbsp (28 g) salted butter, softened at room temperature

¾ cup (180 g) packed brown sugar

½ cup (105 g) granulated sugar

2 large eggs

½ tsp vanilla extract

1½ cups (210 g) all-purpose flour

1 tsp baking soda

½ tsp salt

3 cups (309 g) uncooked old-fashioned whole rolled oats

1 cup (180 g) white chocolate chips

1 cup (170 g) chopped dried apricots

½ cup (45 g) sweetened shredded coconut

½ batch White Chocolate Ganache (page 153; optional)

PREP: Preheat the oven to 350°F (180°C). Spray a 9 x 13-inch (23 x 33-cm) pan with nonstick spray and/or line it with parchment paper.

MAKE THE COOKIE BARS: In a large mixing bowl, cream the softened butter with an electric mixer. Add the brown sugar and granulated sugar and mix well, until creamed together and light and fluffy. Add the eggs and vanilla, and mix until they're just combined. Add the flour, baking soda and salt, and mix until just combined, scraping the sides of the bowl to make sure everything gets incorporated. Add the oats and give the dough a quick mix. Add the white chocolate chips, chopped apricots and coconut, and give another quick mix to distribute the mix-ins throughout the dough.

BAKE: Spread the dough evenly into the prepared pan. You may have to pat it down some to get the dough evenly spread out, but don't pack it in super intensely. Bake for 20 minutes, or until a toothpick inserted into the center comes out clean.

MAKE THE WHITE CHOCOLATE GANACHE AND DECORATE (OPTIONAL): While the bars cool, make half a batch of White Chocolate Ganache (page 153). Let it cool for a few minutes, and then drizzle it over the bars. You don't need to wait until they're completely cool to do this.

SERVE AND STORE: Let the bars cool, then slice and enjoy. You can enjoy them while they're warm if you like, but as always, the longer you let them cool, the better they'll hold a shape when you cut them. Store in an airtight container at room temperature or in the fridge for up to 1 week.

SUPER-THICK
BROWN BUTTER *Brownies*

There's nothing like a good pan of brownies, especially when you need to whip something up for a celebration with minimal ingredients on hand. These take only eight basic ingredients that I bet you have on hand as we speak. Browning the butter is a step that takes just a few extra minutes, but it adds so much flavor to these delightfully fudgy squares.

Yield: 9–18 SQUARES

1 cup (2 sticks or 226 g) salted butter

1½ cups (315 g) granulated sugar

½ cup (120 g) packed brown sugar

4 large eggs

1 tsp vanilla extract

1 cup (140 g) all-purpose flour

⅔ cup (65 g) cocoa powder

½ tsp salt

PREP: Preheat the oven to 350°F (180°C). Spray a 9 x 9-inch (23 x 23-cm) pan with nonstick spray and/or line it with parchment paper.

BROWN THE BUTTER: In a nonstick pan over medium heat, melt the butter. Turn the heat to medium-low and continue cooking the butter, stirring constantly. The butter will get foamy, then bubbly, and then turn golden before turning brown and developing a nutty/caramelly sort of aroma. This will all take about 4 to 6 minutes from the time the butter melts. Once it reaches a deep golden color, immediately remove the pan from the heat, and pour it into a large mixing bowl, scraping the bottom of the pan so you don't leave any of the flavorful brown bits behind.

MAKE THE BROWNIES: Whisk the granulated sugar and brown sugar into the bowl with the browned butter, making sure they're well mixed in. Whisk in the eggs one at a time, and then use the electric mixer to beat the batter for 5 minutes on high speed. (This is what helps develop that nice crinkly crust on top of the brownies.)

Whisk in the vanilla, and then stir in the flour, cocoa and salt, scraping the bowl to make sure everything is mixed in. Give it a few extra stirs, and then spread the batter evenly into the prepared pan.

BAKE: Bake for 35 to 38 minutes, or until a toothpick inserted into the center has a bit of thick batter or thick moist crumbs and is nearly clean when inserted into the edge.

SERVE AND STORE: Let the brownies cool completely before cutting to get neat squares, or dig in while they're still warm from the oven, but let the brownies cool about an hour first to set. Store in an airtight container in the fridge or at room temperature for up to 5 days.

OUR FAVORITE CHILDHOOD
Candy Bars

My brother and I went crazy over these bars when we were kids. In fact, we still do. It's one of those distinctly Midwestern, church potluck type of recipes, and it's incredibly simple to make. These are like a homemade Kit Kat® bar. There are layers of crackers filled with a stovetop brown sugar, caramel-like filling, and the topping is made from peanut butter and chocolate. This recipe makes a TON of bars—perfect for a potluck, or just because you felt like something nostalgic and delicious.

Yield: 16–32 BARS

FOR THE BAR FILLING

1 (13.7-oz [388-g]) box club crackers

2 cups (210 g) graham cracker crumbs

1 cup (2 sticks or 226 g) salted butter

½ cup (105 g) granulated sugar

1 cup (240 g) packed brown sugar

½ cup (120 ml) milk

FOR THE PEANUT BUTTER CHOCOLATE TOPPING

8 oz (226 g) milk chocolate, finely chopped

⅔ cup (187 g) creamy peanut butter

PREP: Spray a 9 x 13–inch (23 x 33–cm) pan with nonstick spray and/or line it with parchment paper. The nonstick spray will help hold the parchment paper in place so it's not jumping around while you are adding the bar layers. Lay down a layer of club crackers to cover the entire bottom of the prepared pan.

MAKE THE FILLING: In a medium pot, add the graham cracker crumbs, butter, granulated sugar, brown sugar and milk. Heat over medium heat until the butter is melted. Turn the heat up a bit to bring the mixture to a boil. Boil for 5 minutes, stirring constantly. Turn the burner off, and remove the pot from the heat. Pour half of the mixture over the crackers in the bottom of the pan. Add another layer of crackers. Pour the remaining half of the filling over the second layer of crackers. Top with a third layer of the club crackers. Set aside.

MAKE THE TOPPING: Add the chocolate and peanut butter to a clean, dry bowl. Microwave in 30-second intervals, stirring between each, until completely melted and smooth. Pour this evenly over the bars.

SERVE AND STORE: Cover and chill the bars in the fridge for at least 2 hours or overnight before slicing. This is a great make-ahead recipe, and the bars will keep in an airtight container in the fridge for 1 week.

Celebratory CAKES AND PIES

There's not an occasion that can't be brightened by a Malted Vanilla Birthday Cake with Chocolate Frosting (page 82), a rich restaurant-level Salted Chocolate Peanut Butter Tart (page 85) or a plate of flaky Caramel Pear Hand Pies (page 75) dripping in 10-Minute Salted Caramel Sauce (page 150). Although some of these desserts may sound fancy and complicated, only one of those things applies here. I've worked to make these recipes as uncomplicated as possible, while keeping that element of a celebration in each of them.

The cakes in this chapter, for instance, are each mixed up in one bowl. With basic recipes like this, there's really no need to mix your dry and wet ingredients separately. So whether you're a beginner or an everyday baker, I know you can make these recipes and still impress folks, whatever the occasion. And, since cakes and pies often require a second element like a crumb topping or a cookie crust, I've used a little trick to keep these recipes to one bowl. Scraping the bowl well (along with a quick wipe from a handy kitchen towel) allows you to keep these recipes one-bowl without sacrificing those extra-special elements, like the crumb layer on the bottom of my Pineapple Upside-Down Crumb Cake (page 77).

There's something in here for each and every celebration—a No-Bake Strawberry Mojito Pie (page 86) for backyard summer parties, a Salted Caramel Apple Galette (page 66) for cozy Friendsgiving and Thanksgiving gatherings and cheerful Raspberry Almond Cupcakes (page 65) for a shower. So whatever the craving, this chapter has something to satisfy it. Sit back, flip through and find inspiration for your next celebration. And honestly, these treats don't even require a celebration in order for you to make them. Make them just because you want to treat yourself. That's celebration enough!

RASPBERRY ALMOND *Cupcakes*

We've all had the traditional wedding cake flavor . . . you know the one. It's a vanilla cake with almond extract added. I've improved that classic flavor to make it even better! These cupcakes start with that same base, but I've added a hint of brown sugar to keep them moist and full of flavor, and I also added raspberry preserves to the frosting and center of these cupcakes for a fun, modern twist.

Yield: 14 CUPCAKES

FOR THE CUPCAKES

½ cup (1 stick or 113 g) salted butter, softened at room temperature

1 cup (210 g) granulated sugar

2 tbsp (26 g) packed brown sugar

3 egg whites, at room temperature

2 tsp (10 ml) vanilla extract

2½ tsp (13 ml) almond extract

½ cup (120 ml) sour cream, at room temperature

½ cup (120 ml) milk, at room temperature

1¾ cups (196 g) spooned and leveled cake flour

¾ tsp baking powder

¼ tsp baking soda

¼ tsp salt

FOR THE RASPBERRY FROSTING AND FILLING

1 (14-oz [397-g]) jar raspberry preserves, divided

1 batch Creamy Vanilla Frosting Base (page 154)

¼ tsp almond extract

PREP: Preheat the oven to 350°F (180°C). Line a cupcake pan with paper liners.

MAKE THE CUPCAKES: In a large mixing bowl, cream the butter with an electric mixer. Add the granulated sugar and brown sugar and mix until well creamed with the butter. Add the egg whites, vanilla extract and almond extract and mix until just combined. It'll look a little lumpy at first but will smooth out as you mix. Add the sour cream and milk, and mix just until they disappear into the batter. Add the flour, baking powder, baking soda and salt, and mix, scraping the sides of the bowl as needed, until the last bits of flour just disappear into the batter. Fill the cupcake liners about three-quarters full.

BAKE: Bake for 16 to 19 minutes. A toothpick inserted into the center will pull out some moist crumbs when the cupcakes are done. Place the cupcake pan on a cooling rack to cool for a few minutes, and then gently use a butter knife or something similar to lift the cupcakes out of the pan. Let the cupcakes continue cooling on the rack until they're completely cool. Never frost a hot or warm cupcake!

MAKE THE FROSTING AND FINISH THE CUPCAKES: Once the cupcakes are cool, use a teaspoon to carve out the center, about halfway down into each cupcake. Add 1 to 2 teaspoons (7 to 14 g) of raspberry preserves into each hole. Make the Creamy Vanilla Frosting Base, according to the directions on page 154, mixing in the almond extract and the remaining ¼ cup (57 g) raspberry preserves last. If it's a particularly warm day and the frosting is a bit less stiff than you'd like it to be, pop it in the fridge for 5 to 10 minutes. Use a piping bag and piping tip, an offset spatula or a butter knife to frost the cupcakes.

SERVE AND STORE: Enjoy immediately. Store leftover cupcakes in an airtight container in the fridge for 3 to 4 days.

Tips You can run eggs under warm water for a few seconds if you forget to pull them out ahead of time.

Use raspberry preserves rather than raspberry fruit spread—preserves are more flavorful!

SALTED CARAMEL APPLE *Galette*

This is like an apple pie but half the work. Galettes are great when you're just getting into the world of pies because there's just one crust, there's no transferring the dough into a pie dish and it's supposed to look rustic. One bite of the tender spiced apples drenched in salted caramel sauce and wrapped up in a buttery, flaky crust will have you swooning.

Yield: 8 SLICES

FOR THE CRUST

1¼ cups (175 g) all-purpose flour, plus extra as needed

¾ tsp salt

1 tsp granulated sugar

½ cup (1 stick or 113 g) cold salted butter

5 tbsp (75 ml) cold water

¼ cup (60 ml) cold full-fat sour cream

FOR THE FILLING

3 medium apples (about 4 cups [420 g] rinsed, peeled and sliced ¼" [6 mm] thick; I used 2 Honeycrisp and 1 Gala)

2 tsp (10 ml) lemon juice

1½ tbsp (12 g) all-purpose flour

¼ cup (60 g) packed brown sugar

1 tsp vanilla extract

1¼ tsp (3 g) cinnamon

¼ tsp nutmeg

⅛ tsp ground cloves

¼ tsp salt

MAKE THE CRUST: In a medium mixing bowl, whisk together the flour, salt and sugar. Cut the butter into tablespoon-sized (14-g) pieces and add them to the dry ingredients. Use a pastry cutter or clean hands to cut the butter into the dry ingredients until you have chunks the size of blueberries—some will be a bit bigger and some a bit smaller. Drizzle in the water and add the sour cream. Toss with a fork until the dough is moistened and the sour cream is mixed in. Gently gather the dough into a ball. If the dough holds when you push it together, it's ready. If it's a bit dry and crumbles apart, add a bit more water, 1 to 2 tablespoons (15 to 30 ml). You can also flick some water onto any dry bits hiding in the bottom of the bowl. Gently flatten the ball of dough into a 1-inch (2.5-cm)-thick disk. It might be a little scrappy looking, but it should hold together.

Wrap the disk tightly in plastic wrap and chill in the freezer for at least 1 hour or in the fridge for at least 2 hours and up to 2 days. The dough can also be frozen for up to 2 months. (Let it thaw in the fridge overnight before using.) If you freeze the dough for 1 hour, and your filling isn't ready yet, move the dough to the fridge so it doesn't freeze solid.

MAKE THE FILLING AND ASSEMBLE THE GALETTE: Start the filling once your dough has chilled or while it's close to being finished, but don't take the dough out yet.

If you're making the filling the same day that you made the crust, you can use the same bowl. Just give it a quick wipe first! Add the apples and the lemon juice, flour, brown sugar, vanilla, cinnamon, nutmeg, cloves and salt. Stir well to combine. If the dough has a few minutes left to chill, you can cover the bowl with a kitchen towel and pop it in the fridge for a few minutes, and then leave it in there while you roll out the dough.

Preheat the oven to 400°F (200°C). Line a large baking sheet with parchment paper or a silicone baking mat.

Flour a countertop. Let the dough sit out for a few minutes before you begin rolling it—just so it's not hard as a rock. If you only chilled it the minimum amount of time, you don't need to do this.

(continued)

1 egg

Generous amount of coarse or raw sugar, for sprinkling on the crust

FOR TOPPING AND FOR SERVING

1 batch 10-Minute Salted Caramel Sauce (page 150) or 1 jar store-bought caramel sauce

Flaky sea salt (optional; I love Maldon brand)

Vanilla ice cream

Unwrap the dough and sprinkle it lightly with flour on top. Sprinkle your rolling pin with flour, too. Begin rolling out the dough gently, turning continuously so it doesn't stick to the counter. Sprinkle more flour under the dough as needed. If the dough has some cracks in it, flip it over and work with the other side for a bit. Be a little patient here. We're not trying to stretch the dough all the way out in a few passes of the rolling pin.

Once the dough is about 12 to 14 inches (30 to 36 cm) in diameter and about ⅛ inch (3 mm) thick, gently roll it up onto the rolling pin and transfer it onto the prepared baking sheet. Evenly spread the apple filling onto the dough, leaving a 2- to 3-inch (5- to 8-cm) border around the edges. You can fan the apple slices out in circles, or you can just let them fall where they fall. Just try to keep them from piling up super unevenly in the galette. Drizzle the liquid left in the bottom of the bowl over the apple slices.

Fold up the edges, working in small sections at a time, covering the edges of the apples a bit. Galettes are meant to be rustic—don't fuss over trying to make it look perfect. Chill the assembled galette, uncovered, in the fridge for 15 minutes. This is important as the dough will have warmed a bit from working with it, and we want it nice and cold when it goes into the oven so it holds its shape.

Beat the egg in a measuring cup you already used. Once the galette has chilled, brush the egg wash over the exposed areas of the crust. Sprinkle some coarse or raw sugar over the crust as well.

BAKE: Bake for 38 to 40 minutes. The crust will be golden brown and should feel crisp if you tap on it carefully with a fingertip. You can also prick the apples with a fork to make sure they're tender.

SERVE AND STORE: Brush the apple slices in the galette with a little of the 10-Minute Salted Caramel Sauce when it comes out of the oven. Let it rest about 10 minutes before slicing and serving. Drizzle slices with more salted caramel sauce and flaky sea salt, and serve with vanilla ice cream. This is best while it's fresh and warm, but you can keep leftovers in the fridge for 2 to 3 days in an airtight container.

APPLE SNACKING *Cake* WITH OAT CRUMBLE

I fell in love with this cake after my first bite. We've got a spiced, fluffy layer of cake on the bottom, a layer of caramelized apples on top of that and it's all capped off with an oat streusel and a dusting of powdered sugar. Perfect for a picnic, a potluck or an afternoon snack you can whip up after your annual autumn apple-picking excursion.

Yield: 8–16 SLICES

FOR THE APPLE FILLING

3 tbsp (42 g) salted butter

2 large Golden Delicious apples (about 1 lb [454 g]), sliced into ¼" (6-mm) slices

2 tbsp (26 g) granulated sugar

1 tbsp (13 g) packed brown sugar

¾ tsp cinnamon

Pinch of salt

FOR THE CAKE

¼ cup (½ stick or 57 g) salted butter, softened at room temperature

½ cup (105 g) granulated sugar

¼ cup (60 g) packed brown sugar

1 large egg

½ cup (120 ml) milk

1 tsp vanilla extract

1½ cups (210 g) all-purpose flour

2 tsp (8 g) baking powder

¼ tsp salt

½ tsp cinnamon

¼ tsp nutmeg

Pinch of ground cloves

PREP: Preheat the oven to 350°F (180°C). Spray a 9-inch (23-cm) cake pan with nonstick spray and line with parchment paper.

MAKE THE FILLING: Melt the butter in a large saucepan. Add the apples, granulated sugar, brown sugar, cinnamon and salt, and cook for 8 minutes over medium to medium-high heat, stirring gently the whole time. The apples will soften and become caramelized. Turn off the heat when the time is up, and move the pan to a different burner so the apples can cool a bit while you make the cake.

MAKE THE CAKE: In a large mixing bowl, cream the softened butter with an electric mixer. Add the granulated sugar and brown sugar, and mix until well creamed with the butter. Add the egg, milk and vanilla, and mix until just combined. Add the flour, baking powder, salt, cinnamon, nutmeg and cloves, and mix again, scraping the sides of the bowl to get everything incorporated. Stop mixing just as the last streaks of flour disappear into the batter. Spread the batter evenly into the prepared cake pan, using your spatula to get all of the batter out of the bowl. Evenly spread the caramelized apples in a layer over the cake batter.

(continued)

FOR THE TOPPING AND FOR SERVING

¾ cup (105 g) all-purpose flour

⅓ cup (33 g) rolled oats

½ cup (105 g) granulated sugar

Pinch of salt

¼ tsp cinnamon

Pinch of nutmeg

Pinch of ground cloves

6 tbsp (85 g) cold salted butter

Dusting of powdered sugar

1 batch 10-Minute Salted Caramel Sauce (page 150; optional)

MAKE THE TOPPING: Give the bowl a quick wipe with a kitchen towel if there are still some patches of batter in it. Add the flour, oats, sugar, salt, cinnamon, nutmeg and cloves, and whisk to combine them. Cut the cold butter into tablespoon-sized (14-g) chunks, and cut it into the dry ingredients with a pastry cutter or clean hands until you have very small pieces (pea-size and smaller) scattered throughout the topping. Evenly spread the topping over the apple layer.

BAKE AND SERVE: Bake for 45 to 48 minutes. A toothpick inserted into the center will come out clean or with a few moist crumbs. Let the cake cool in the cake pan on a cooling rack for about 20 minutes before lifting it out using the parchment paper. Let it cool a bit more on the cooling rack before slicing and serving with a dusting of powdered sugar. This also pairs wonderfully with my 10-Minute Salted Caramel Sauce (page 150).

Pumpkin Pie WITH GINGERSNAP PRESS-IN CRUST

Everyone loves pumpkin pie, but this is the best one, if I do say so myself. The crushed cookie crust is simpler and quicker to make than homemade pie crust—perfect in a pinch and perfect for bakers who aren't confident working with pie dough. Not only is this pie a breeze to make, but it has the most flavorful filling!

Yield: 8 SLICES

FOR THE CRUST

4½ tbsp (64 g) salted butter

1½ cups (150 g) gingersnap cookie crumbs

1 tbsp (13 g) packed brown sugar

Pinch of salt

FOR THE FILLING

1¼ cups (300 g) pumpkin puree

1 cup (240 ml) evaporated milk

1 large egg

½ tsp vanilla extract

2 tbsp (30 ml) real maple syrup

½ cup plus 1 tbsp (138 g) packed brown sugar

¼ tsp salt

1½ tsp (4 g) cinnamon

¾ tsp ground ginger

¼ tsp cloves

¼ tsp nutmeg

¼ tsp allspice

2 tsp (6 g) cornstarch

Pinch of black pepper

FOR THE TOPPING

1 batch Classic Vanilla Whipped Cream (page 158)

PREP: Preheat the oven to 350°F (180°C). Spray a 9-inch (23-cm) pie dish with nonstick spray.

MAKE AND BAKE THE CRUST: Melt the butter in a large mixing bowl in the microwave, and then stir in the gingersnap cookie crumbs, the sugar and a pinch of salt. Press the crust evenly into your prepared pie dish and up the sides, making sure to scrape the bowl well.

Bake the crust for 10 minutes. Set aside while you mix up the filling.

MAKE THE FILLING AND BAKE THE PIE: Lower the oven temperature to 325°F (165°C). To use the same bowl from the crust, give it a quick wipe to remove any leftover crust crumbs. Add the pumpkin, evaporated milk, egg, vanilla and maple syrup. Whisk together well. Whisk in the sugar, salt, cinnamon, ginger, cloves, nutmeg, allspice, cornstarch and pepper, making sure no clumps of sugar or anything else are hiding in the bottom of the bowl. Pour into the prepared crust.

Bake the pie for 52 to 54 minutes. The center should seem just set, and a toothpick inserted into the center will be mostly clean with a few small bits of thick filling, and a knife inserted into the center will have a bit of thick filling on it.

SERVE AND STORE: Let the pie cool at room temperature for at least 4 hours before slicing and serving; however, it's best after it's chilled in the fridge overnight. Serve with 1 batch of Classic Vanilla Whipped Cream (page 158). The pie can be made 1 to 2 days ahead of time, cooled at room temperature, and then stored in the fridge, covered, until ready to serve. Leftovers can be stored in the fridge, covered, for 4 to 5 days.

CARAMEL PEAR *Hand Pies*

Hand pies are just about the best dessert I know how to make. They've got everything we love about a pie—a crisp, buttery, flaky crust and a delicious spiced pear filling—but, they're handheld, and this is a great starting point if you're not someone who bakes full pies very often. You won't have to worry about transferring pie dough to a pie dish or spending extra time fussing with a latticed top crust. These are a wonderful fall baking project, a fun alternative to a traditional pie at Thanksgiving or a fun treat to serve on Halloween.

Yield: 18 HAND PIES

FOR THE CRUST

3 cups (420 g) all-purpose flour, plus more as needed

¾ tsp salt

1 tbsp (13 g) granulated sugar

1 cup (2 sticks or 226 g) plus 2 tbsp (28 g) cold salted butter

15 to 20 tbsp (225 to 300 ml) cold water

FOR THE FILLING

4 medium, ripe Bartlett pears, diced into 1-inch (2.5-cm) pieces (about 3 cups [365 g])

1½ tbsp (21 g) salted butter

⅓ cup (80 g) packed brown sugar

½ tsp ground ginger

1¼ tsp (3 g) cinnamon

¼ tsp nutmeg

⅛ tsp ground cloves

Pinch of salt

1 egg

MAKE THE CRUST: In a large mixing bowl, whisk together the flour, salt, and sugar. Cut the butter into tablespoon-sized (14 g) cubes, and add them to the dry ingredients. Use a pastry cutter or clean hands to cut the butter into the dry ingredients until you have pieces of butter the size of walnut halves—some will be a bit bigger and some a bit smaller.

Drizzle in 5 tablespoons (75 ml) of the cold water. Toss with a fork to mix this in, and then repeat two more times. Gently gather the dough into a ball. If the dough holds when you push it together, it's ready. If it's a bit dry and crumbles apart, add 1 to 5 tablespoons (15 to 75 ml) extra water, 1 tablespoon (15 ml) at a time. You want the dough to hold together without being dry, but it shouldn't be sticky either. Flick some water onto any dry bits hiding in the bottom of the bowl.

Once the dough is in a ball, slice it in half with a knife. Gently flatten each half into a 1-inch (2.5-cm)-thick disk. Push any crumbly bits into place as best you can, and try to make sure there isn't a fissure in the disk that is causing it to fall apart. It may be a little scrappy looking, but it should hold together.

Wrap each disk tightly in plastic wrap and chill in the freezer for at least 1 hour or in the fridge for at least 2 hours and up to 3 days. The dough can also be frozen up to 2 months—let it thaw in the fridge overnight before using. If you freeze the dough for 1 hour, and your filling isn't ready yet, move the dough to the fridge so it doesn't freeze solid on you.

MAKE THE FILLING: Add the pears, butter, brown sugar, ginger, cinnamon, nutmeg, cloves and salt to a medium pot over medium heat and stir to combine. Cook for 3 minutes; the butter will be melted and the pears should be softened but not mushy. Remove from the heat and let the filling hang out in the pan while you roll out the dough.

ASSEMBLE THE HAND PIES: Line a few baking sheets with parchment paper or silicone baking mats.

Get out one of the dough disks and leave the other in the fridge for now. I like to work with one at a time, and once the first baking sheet of pies is in the oven, I start the process over with the next dough disk.

(continued)

FOR THE TOPPING

Coarse sugar

1 batch 10-Minute Salted Caramel Sauce (page 150) or 1 jar store-bought caramel sauce

Flaky sea salt (optional; I love Maldon brand)

Tips *If you chilled your dough longer than the minimum time, you may need to let it sit for a few minutes at room temperature before rolling it out. If it's cracking a lot as you try to roll it, this is why. I find that I don't have to do this often, but it's a tip for ya!*

Use the scraps from your final roll-out to make pie crust "chips." Cut the scraps into semi-uniform pieces and brush them with egg wash, then sprinkle with cinnamon sugar. Bake for about 20 minutes, or until deep golden brown and crisp.

Hand pies can be fully assembled, leaving off the egg wash, and frozen. Freeze them on a baking sheet first so they don't stick together, then freeze them in an airtight container for up to 2 months. Bake them from frozen, following all the same directions in the recipe.

Flour your counter and rolling pin. Start in the center of the disk and gently roll the dough out in all directions. Turn the dough every few rolls to make sure it's not sticking to the counter. Lightly re-flour the counter and sprinkle a little more flour on the dough if it is sticking. Push together any cracked areas and continue rolling. Roll the dough out to about 14 x 14 inches (36 x 36 cm) and about ⅛ inch (3 mm) thick. (It doesn't have to be perfect.)

Cut out circles using a round cookie cutter or drinking glass. (My cutter was 3½ inches [9 cm] across.) Gently gather the scraps together into a ball. Wrap it back up in the plastic wrap, and pop it in the fridge for a quick re-chill while you assemble the first round of hand pies.

Arrange half of the circles on your prepared baking sheets. I can usually fit six to seven pies on a standard cookie sheet, and each dough disk will give you about 12 pieces on the first roll-outs. These are your bottom crusts. Beat the egg with a fork in a used measuring cup for your egg wash. Brush the egg wash around the edges of the dough circles.

Place about 1 tablespoon (15 g) of filling in the center of each circle. Place another circle over the filling. Use your fingertip to seal the pieces of dough together, by pressing the top edge into the bottom edge all the way around the circle. It's okay if some filling leaks out.

Cover the baking sheet with a kitchen towel, and pop it in the fridge for 20 minutes or in the freezer for 10 minutes. This will help re-chill the dough before baking so it bakes nicely and holds its shape.

BAKE: Preheat the oven to 375°F (190°C).

Use the tines of a fork to crimp all around the edges of the pies. Lightly brush the hand pies with the egg wash. Use a fork to poke an "X" into the tops. Sprinkle with a little coarse sugar.

Bake for 24 to 28 minutes, or until the pies are a nice golden brown. Let the pies cool on the baking sheet for 10 minutes.

While one batch bakes, pull the second dough disk out of the fridge, roll it out and repeat this process. Repeat again with the dough scraps from each dough disk, and then one last time, combining the dough scraps for the third and final roll out. See Tips for a way to use the remaining dough scraps.

SERVE AND STORE: Serve warm or cooled (I prefer them nice and warm), and drizzle with my 10-Minute Salted Caramel Sauce. You can even add a sprinkle of flaky sea salt. These are best while they're fresh, but leftovers can be stored in an airtight container in the fridge for 2 to 3 days.

PINEAPPLE UPSIDE-DOWN
Crumb Cake

I've elevated this pineapple upside-down cake a smidge by adding a surprise crumb layer on the bottom. It's such a beautiful contrast to bite into the crunchy layer at the bottom of the fluffy cake with the juicy, sweet pineapple on top. The pineapple layer comes together in the cake pan, eliminating the need for an extra bowl to prepare the topping!

Yield: 8 SLICES

FOR THE PINEAPPLE LAYER

¼ cup (½ stick or 57 g) salted butter, plus additional for greasing the pan

½ cup (120 g) packed brown sugar

Rings from 1 large pineapple (about 1 lb [454 g]), sliced into quarters

Handful of maraschino cherries

FOR THE CAKE

½ cup (1 stick or 113 g) salted butter, softened at room temperature

1 cup (210 g) granulated sugar

2 tbsp (25 g) packed brown sugar

2 large eggs

2 tsp (10 ml) vanilla extract

1⅔ cups (234 g) all-purpose flour

1½ tsp (7 g) baking powder

¼ tsp salt

¼ tsp cinnamon

1 cup (240 ml) full-fat Greek yogurt

1 tbsp (15 ml) milk

PREP: Preheat the oven to 350°F (180°C).

MAKE THE PINEAPPLE LAYER: Grease a 9-inch (23-cm) round cake pan well with a knob of butter, making sure to get into the edges, and then add the ¼ cup (½ stick or 57 g) butter to the pan. Pop the pan in the oven while it preheats, just until the butter is melted. Remove the pan from the oven, and spray a little cooking spray on the sides of the inside of the pan for extra insurance. Sprinkle the brown sugar evenly over the melted butter in the pan, and then arrange the pineapple pieces on top. Add a few maraschino cherries into any gaps between the pineapple pieces. Set aside.

MAKE THE CAKE: In a large bowl, cream the butter with an electric mixer. Add the granulated sugar and brown sugar, and mix until creamed together. Add the eggs and vanilla, and mix until just combined. Add the flour, baking powder, salt and cinnamon. Mix until just combined, scraping the sides of the bowl as needed. Add the Greek yogurt and the milk, and mix until the last streaks of milk and yogurt disappear into the batter. Pour the thick batter over the pineapple in the cake pan, and smooth it into an even layer. Scrape the bowl well to get all the batter out, and then give it a quick wipe with a clean kitchen towel.

(continued)

FOR THE CRUMB LAYER

¼ cup (½ stick or 57 g) salted butter

½ cup plus 1 tbsp (80 g) all-purpose flour

¼ cup (53 g) granulated sugar

2 tsp (5 g) raw turbinado sugar (optional—it gives a nice crunch! Or use 2 tsp [9 g] more granulated sugar if you don't have this)

Pinch of salt

Pinch of cinnamon

FOR THE TOPPING

1 batch Classic Vanilla Whipped Cream (page 158)

Maraschino cherries (optional)

MAKE THE CRUMB LAYER: Melt the butter in the same large bowl you used to make the cake. Add the flour, granulated sugar, turbinado sugar, salt and cinnamon. Stir together. Sprinkle this mixture, breaking it up into crumbs, over the cake batter.

BAKE: Bake for 60 to 62 minutes. When done, a toothpick inserted into the center of the cake will come out clean. Let the cake cool in the pan for 10 minutes, and then run a knife around the edge to loosen. Invert the cake onto a cooling rack. If the cake seems to be sticking, gently but firmly tap on the bottom of the cake pan with the end of a butter knife while the cake pan is flipped upside down on the cooling rack.

SERVE AND STORE: Let the cake cool before cutting and serving. Serve with Classic Vanilla Whipped Cream (page 158) and maraschino cherries, if desired. Store leftovers in the fridge for 3 to 4 days in an airtight container, but this is really best the first day.

BUTTERBEER *Cupcakes*

I was always fascinated with the food in the books I read growing up, and I loved making "concoctions," as my mom affectionately called them, in our kitchen as a kid. This isn't a weird concoction, never fear, but it is my take on what a butterbeer-flavored dessert from our favorite childhood series would taste like. These little cakes are flavored with butterscotch, cream soda and butter extract, and the whole thing is a sweet, buttery, caramelly dream.

Yield: **16 CUPCAKES**

FOR THE CUPCAKES

½ cup (1 stick or 113 g) salted butter, softened at room temperature

1 cup (240 g) packed brown sugar

3 egg whites

1 tsp vanilla extract

2½ tsp (13 ml) butter extract

½ cup (120 ml) sour cream, at room temperature

¾ cup (180 ml) cream soda, at room temperature

1¾ cups (196 g) cake flour, spooned and leveled

½ tsp baking powder

¼ tsp baking soda

¼ tsp salt

1 (3.4-oz [96-g]) package instant butterscotch pudding mix (not cook and serve)

FOR THE BUTTERBEER FROSTING

1 batch Creamy Vanilla Frosting Base (page 154)

2 tbsp (30 ml) cream soda, in place of the milk

1 (3.4-oz [96-g]) package instant butterscotch pudding mix

Sprinkles, for decorating (optional)

PREP: Preheat the oven to 350°F (180°C). Line a cupcake pan with paper cupcake liners.

MAKE THE CUPCAKES: In a large mixing bowl, cream the butter with an electric mixer. Add the brown sugar and mix until well creamed with the butter. Add the egg whites and mix until just combined. Add the vanilla, butter extract, sour cream and cream soda, and mix until just combined. Add the cake flour, baking powder, baking soda and salt, and mix until just combined, scraping the sides of the bowl as needed. Add the butterscotch pudding mix, dry, from the box. Mix until combined. Fill the cupcake liners about three-quarters of the way full.

Bake for 18 to 20 minutes. A toothpick inserted into the center will pull some moist crumbs out, but you shouldn't see any wet batter. Let the cupcakes cool for a few minutes in the pan, and then use a spoon or a butter knife to gently lift them out and transfer to a cooling rack. Let the cupcakes cool completely before frosting.

MAKE THE FROSTING AND FROST THE CUPCAKES: Once the cupcakes are cool, make the Creamy Vanilla Frosting Base according to the directions on page 154, subbing the cream soda for the milk. Mix in the dry butterscotch pudding mix last.

Frost the cupcakes using a piping bag, offset spatula or a butter knife. If you frost them while they're warm, the frosting will melt right off. Top with sprinkles, if you like.

SERVE AND STORE: Enjoy the cupcakes once they've been frosted. Store leftovers in an airtight container in the fridge for 3 to 4 days.

> *Tip* Use a fresh can or bottle of cream soda that hasn't already been opened. It needs to have its full fizz!

MALTED VANILLA *Birthday Cake*
WITH CHOCOLATE FROSTING

I've amped up my favorite cake here—yellow cake with chocolate frosting—by adding malt powder to both the cake and the frosting. It's such a unique (and addicting) flavor. Keeping the cake to a single layer ensures that this recipe is simple enough for you to bake over and over, for any and all occasions.

Yield: 9 SLICES

FOR THE CAKE

Shortening, for greasing pan

All-purpose flour, for greasing pan

½ cup (1 stick or 113 g) salted butter, softened at room temperature

1¼ cups (265 g) granulated sugar

3½ large eggs (see directions at right)

2 tsp (10 ml) vanilla extract

1⅓ cups (150 g) cake flour, spooned and leveled

¼ tsp salt

¼ tsp baking powder

¼ tsp baking soda

¾ cup plus 2 tbsp (140 g) malt powder

3 tbsp (45 ml) vegetable oil

½ cup (120 ml) full-fat Greek yogurt

FOR THE FROSTING

1 batch Creamy Vanilla Frosting Base (page 154)

¼ cup (40 g) malt powder

½ cup plus 1 tbsp (56 g) cocoa powder

Crushed Whoppers candies, for decorating (optional)

PREP: Preheat the oven to 325°F (165°C). Grease and flour a 9-inch (23-cm) square baking dish. To do this, use shortening—spread it around the entire inside of the dish with a paper towel. Then, sprinkle a handful or two of flour inside the pan and tap the sides of the pan to move it around, so it coats the entire inside of the pan. Tap out any excess flour.

MAKE THE CAKE: In a large mixing bowl, cream the softened butter with an electric mixer. Add the sugar and mix until well creamed. Measure half an egg by beating 1 egg in a measuring cup with a fork and measuring out 2 tablespoons (30 ml)—that's half an egg. Discard the second half or save it for another recipe. Add the eggs and vanilla and mix until just combined. Add the cake flour, salt, baking powder, baking soda and malt powder, mixing until the last traces of the dry ingredients just disappear into the batter. Scrape the sides of the bowl to make sure everything gets mixed in. Add the vegetable oil and Greek yogurt, and mix until just combined.

Pour the batter in to the prepared pan, spreading it evenly. Bake for 54 to 57 minutes. A toothpick inserted into the center should be clean or have some moist crumbs. Let the cake cool in the pan on a cooling rack on your counter for 10 minutes. Run a butter knife around the edges to loosen, and then invert the cake onto the cooling rack. Let the cake cool completely before frosting it.

SERVE AND STORE: Make the Creamy Vanilla Frosting Base according to the directions on page 154, mixing in the malt powder and cocoa powder last. Spread the frosting on the cooled cake, and sprinkle with crushed Whopper candies, if desired. Slice and serve. Store leftovers in an airtight container in the fridge for 5 to 6 days. Let the leftover slices come back to room temperature a bit before enjoying.

> *Make-Ahead Tip* The cake can be made a day ahead, cooled completely and stored in an airtight container at room temperature for a day before frosting and serving.

SALTED CHOCOLATE PEANUT BUTTER *Tart*

This dessert was inspired by an incredible dessert my husband, Grant, and I had on a trip to Colorado. Everyone will think it's a restaurant dessert when you serve it, but you won't have to spend all day in the kitchen to pull it off. It's got a crunchy, salty peanut crust, a thick layer of peanut butter mousse and a smooth layer of chocolate ganache. You MUST top this with crushed peanuts and flaky sea salt. It's a salty-sweet lover's dream dessert!

Yield: 8 LARGE OR 16 SMALLER SLICES

FOR THE CRUST

1½ cups (228 g) peanuts (I use the lightly salted cocktail type)

½ cup (1 stick or 113 g) salted butter

¾ cup (105 g) all-purpose flour

⅛ tsp salt

2 tbsp (26 g) granulated sugar

½ tsp baking powder

FOR THE FILLING

¾ cup (180 ml) cold heavy cream

4 oz (113 g) cream cheese, softened at room temperature

1 cup (260 g) creamy peanut butter

½ cup (105 g) granulated sugar

2 tsp (10 ml) vanilla extract

½ tsp salt, plus an extra pinch

FOR THE TOPPING

1 batch Chocolate Ganache (page 153)

Peanuts, as desired

Flaky sea salt (I love Maldon brand)

PREP: Preheat the oven to 350°F (180°C). Spray a round 9-inch (23-cm) tart pan or cake pan with nonstick spray. I like to use a tart pan here because the removable bottom makes it easier to cut and serve neat slices, but you can, of course, use a cake pan if that's what you have.

MAKE THE CRUST: Pulse the peanuts in a food processor just until they're roughly chopped. Don't let it run too long or you'll make peanut butter. Melt the butter in a medium mixing bowl in the microwave. Stir in the peanuts, flour, salt, sugar and baking powder. Scrape the bowl really well to get all the crust bits out, and press the crust evenly into and up the sides of the tart pan. Bake for 9 minutes. Set aside to cool completely while you make the filling.

MAKE THE FILLING: Give the mixing bowl a quick wipe with a kitchen towel if there are still crust pieces in it. Measure the cold heavy cream into the bowl using a 1- or 2-cup (240- to 480-ml) glass measuring cup. Beat the heavy cream with an electric mixer on high speed just until softly whipped—we're not going for stiff peaks here. Pour the softly whipped cream back into the measuring cup you used to measure it. Pop this in the fridge while you finish making the filling. Add the cream cheese to the same bowl, and beat on high speed until creamed. Add the peanut butter, sugar, vanilla and salt, and mix until well combined. Add about one-third (just eyeball it) of the whipped cream into the bowl with the filling, and mix until just combined. Add the rest of the whipped cream and gently fold it in with a silicone spatula until it's completely combined.

If the crust is still cooling, cover the bowl with a kitchen towel and pop it in the fridge until the crust is cool.

Spread the peanut butter filling into the cooled crust. Pop in the fridge while you make the ganache. Make the Chocolate Ganache as directed on page 153. Let it cool for a few minutes more, and then pour over the tart.

SERVE AND STORE: Let the tart chill in the fridge for at least 6 hours or overnight before serving. Serve with a sprinkle of peanuts and flaky sea salt. Store leftovers in an airtight container in the fridge for 5 or 6 days.

NO-BAKE STRAWBERRY MOJITO *Pie*

No-bake desserts are everyone's favorite during the hot summer months—especially if you live in Wisconsin where it's regularly 90 degrees with 90-percent humidity. This pie is a breeze to whip up with no heat required. It's light and a little tart, and the flavors of strawberry, lime and rum are perfectly refreshing.

Yield: 8–16 SLICES

FOR THE CRUST

½ cup (1 stick or 113 g) salted butter

2 cups (215 g) graham cracker crumbs

2 tbsp (26 g) granulated sugar

FOR THE FILLING

12 oz (345 g) full-fat block-style cream cheese

⅔ cup (80 g) powdered sugar

⅓ cup (80 ml) key lime juice

⅓ cup (80 ml) rum

1 tsp lime zest

1¼ cups (394 g) strawberry preserves

1 (8-oz [226-g] container whipped topping, thawed (do this in the fridge, overnight)

FOR THE TOPPING

1 batch Classic Vanilla Whipped Cream (page 158)

1 tsp key lime juice

Lime slices and/or lime zest, to garnish

PREP: Spray a 9½-inch (24-cm) deep pie dish with nonstick spray.

MAKE THE CRUST: Melt the butter in a large mixing bowl in the microwave. Stir in the graham cracker crumbs and sugar. Press the crust evenly into the pie plate and up the sides. Scrape the bowl well to get all the crumbs out, and give it a quick wipe with a kitchen towel. Put the crust in the fridge to chill while you make the filling.

MAKE THE FILLING: Cream the cream cheese in the same large mixing bowl with an electric mixer. Add the powdered sugar and mix until well combined with the cream cheese. Add the key lime juice, rum, lime zest and strawberry preserves. Mix. It's going to look curdled and weird, but just keep mixing on high for 1 minute or so until it smooths out. Fold in the whipped topping with a silicone spatula until it's all mixed in with the rest of the filling. Spread the filling into the crust, and freeze for at least 6 hours before slicing and serving.

SERVE AND STORE: Make the Classic Vanilla Whipped Cream (page 158), adding the key lime juice along with the other whipped cream ingredients. Top the pie with the whipped cream, lime slices and/or lime zest. Enjoy! Keep leftovers, covered, in the freezer for 1 to 2 weeks.

CRISPS, COBBLERS
and A PANDOWDY

I'm a lover of all things cobblers, crisps and even pandowdies. Tall, flaky, sweet biscuits (Blueberry Cobbler for Two [page 105]); cinnamon-sugared puff pastry stars (Caramel Peach Pandowdy [page 98]); or a classic brown sugar and cinnamon crisp topping (Strawberry Rhubarb Crisp [page 102])—there's just something so magical about the fruit fillings that cook underneath these perfect complementary toppings. And we can't forget the fillings: a bourbon-spiked sweet cherry filling in my Brown Sugar and Bourbon Cherry Crisp (page 93); spiced cranberries, pears and apples that taste just like everything you love about a nostalgic Thanksgiving in my Spiced Cranberry, Pear and Apple Crisp (page 90); a five-berry filling that's summer encapsulated in my Everything but the Kitchen Sink Mixed Berry Cobbler (page 94); and a filling of juicy peaches swimming in salted caramel sauce in my Caramel Peach Pandowdy (page 98). How could I ever choose just one? Good thing I got to make and eat them all many, many times while writing this book.

All of these recipes (with the exception of the Double Chocolate Cobbler [page 101]) have a fruit filling that gets tossed together in the dish you'll bake it in. Talk about ease! The toppings vary, but they're all quite simple too. Oh, and since I've singled it out, let's dive into that Double Chocolate Cobbler (literally AND figuratively). It's a brownie-like batter that gets mixed up and poured into a pan, and then we top it with brown sugar, cocoa powder and hot water. It bakes into the most beautiful, decadent dessert that's like a huge chocolate lava cake in a pan.

So whether you're partial to chocolate or fruit, a small or a large batch, there is something in this chapter for you.

SPICED CRANBERRY, PEAR AND APPLE *Crisp*

Tender spiced apples, pears and cranberries are nestled underneath a mountain of the most perfect buttery, brown sugar crisp topping. This dessert tastes exactly like your fondest Thanksgiving memories—it's fall and nostalgia encapsulated.

 **Yield: 4-6 SERVINGS**

FOR THE FRUIT FILLING

½ cup plus 1 tbsp (138 g) packed brown sugar

⅓ cup (45 g) all-purpose flour

2 medium Bartlett pears (about 2½ cups [400 g]), sliced into ¼" (6-mm)-thick slices

2 medium apples (about 2½ cups [315 g]), peeled and sliced into ¼" (6-mm)-thick slices

1 cup (105 g) frozen whole cranberries

1 tsp cinnamon

¼ tsp nutmeg

⅛ tsp salt

½ tsp vanilla extract

FOR THE TOPPING AND FOR SERVING

½ cup plus 1 tbsp (80 g) all-purpose flour

¾ cup (180 g) packed brown sugar

½ tsp cinnamon

¼ tsp salt

½ cup (1 stick or 113 g) plus 1 tbsp (14 g) cold salted butter

1 cup (98 g) old-fashioned whole rolled oats

Vanilla ice cream or Classic Vanilla Whipped Cream (page 158)

PREP: Preheat the oven to 350°F (180°C). Get out a 9-inch (23-cm) baking dish.

MAKE THE FILLING: Whisk together the brown sugar and flour in the bottom of the baking dish. Add the pear and apple slices, frozen cranberries, cinnamon, nutmeg, salt and vanilla, and toss well with a silicone spatula, making sure to get any chunks of floury sugar that are hiding in the bottom. Set aside.

MAKE THE TOPPING: In a medium mixing bowl, whisk together the flour, brown sugar, cinnamon and salt. Cut the cold butter into the dry ingredients using a pastry cutter or clean hands, until you have pieces of butter blueberry-size and smaller. Stir in the oats. Give the fruit filling one more good stir, and then sprinkle the topping evenly over the top.

BAKE: Bake for 45 minutes. The filling will be bubbly and the crisp topping will be golden brown. You can stick a fork through the topping to pierce the apples and make sure they're tender. Add 2 to 4 more minutes to the baking time if the apples don't feel tender enough.

SERVE AND STORE: Let the crisp rest about 10 minutes before serving. Enjoy with vanilla ice cream, Classic Vanilla Whipped Cream (page 158) or on its own. This crisp is best when it's warm from the oven, but leftovers can be stored in an airtight container in the fridge for 3 to 4 days. The topping won't be as crisp after the first day—so I don't recommend making this ahead at all.

> *Tip* I prefer to use Pink Lady, Honeycrisp, or Gala apples for this recipe!

BROWN SUGAR AND BOURBON CHERRY *Crisp*

This cherry crisp is just heavenly! The filling is made with dark sweet cherries spiked with bourbon and flavored with brown sugar and a little orange juice, and the topping is the perfect crisp topping—buttery and full of brown sugar, oats and a pinch of orange zest. This makes the perfect date-night dessert or the perfect treat to share with a friend.

Yield: 2–3 SERVINGS

FOR THE FILLING

14½ oz (412 g) dark sweet cherries, rinsed, pitted and halved (about 2⅔ cups)

3 tbsp (40 g) granulated sugar

1 tbsp (13 g) packed brown sugar

3½ tbsp (28 g) cornstarch

½ tsp vanilla extract

2 tbsp (30 ml) bourbon

1 tsp orange juice

½ tsp orange zest

FOR THE TOPPING AND FOR SERVING

¼ cup plus 1 tbsp (53 g) all-purpose flour

⅓ cup plus 1 tbsp (95 g) packed brown sugar

¼ tsp cinnamon

¼ tsp orange zest

¼ tsp salt

4½ tbsp (64 g) cold salted butter

½ cup (50 g) old-fashioned whole rolled oats

Vanilla ice cream or Classic Vanilla Whipped Cream (page 158)

PREP: Preheat the oven to 350°F (180°C). Spray a 6-inch (15-cm) baking dish with nonstick spray.

MAKE THE FILLING: Add the cherries, granulated sugar, brown sugar and cornstarch to the baking dish, and stir well to combine. Add the vanilla, bourbon, orange juice and zest, and stir to combine.

MAKE THE TOPPING: In a medium bowl, whisk together the flour, brown sugar, cinnamon, orange zest and salt. Cut in the butter with a pastry cutter until you have pea-sized chunks scattered throughout. Stir in the oats. Sprinkle the topping evenly over the cherry filling.

BAKE: Bake for 45 to 48 minutes. The filling will be bubbly and the topping will be golden brown. You can also poke the fruit through the topping with a fork. The cherries should feel tender. Let sit for about 10 minutes before digging in.

SERVE AND STORE: Enjoy warm with vanilla ice cream or Classic Vanilla Whipped Cream (page 158). This is best enjoyed when it's fresh from the oven, but you can store leftovers covered in the fridge for 2 to 3 days.

EVERYTHING BUT THE KITCHEN SINK MIXED BERRY *Cobbler*

This berry cobbler uses five—yes, five!—types of berries for the most delicious flavor explosion. The filling is juicy and full of blackberries, strawberries, blueberries, cherries and raspberries—and the biscuits on top are tall and fluffy. The whole thing is the perfect marriage of biscuit topping and fruit filling—and it's all made even easier by stirring together the fruit filling in the pan. Happy cobbling!

Yield: **6 SERVINGS**

FOR THE BERRY FILLING

1½ cups frozen (210 g) or fresh (228 g) strawberries (if using fresh, rinse and quarter them)

1½ cups (220 g) frozen or fresh dark sweet cherries (if using fresh, rinse, pit and halve them)

1 cup frozen (130 g) or fresh (150 g) blackberries

1 cup (145 g) frozen or fresh blueberries

1 cup frozen (125 g) or fresh (150 g) raspberries

½ cup (105 g) granulated sugar

¼ cup (35 g) all-purpose flour

2 tsp (10 ml) vanilla extract

¼ tsp cinnamon

1 tsp lemon juice

1 tsp lemon zest

PREP: Preheat the oven to 400°F (200°C). If you're using frozen fruit, do not thaw any of it!

MAKE THE COBBLER: Add all the fruit to a 10-inch (25-cm) oven-safe skillet or baking dish with the remaining filling ingredients. Stir everything together well, so there aren't any big dry clumps of flour or sugar left behind. Set aside.

MIX UP THE BISCUITS: In a medium bowl, whisk together the flour, baking powder, salt, cinnamon and sugar. Cut the butter into the dry ingredients, using a pastry cutter or clean hands, until you have pieces of butter about the size of blueberries or walnut halves. Pour in the buttermilk, and stir until a dough forms. If there are some dry bits in the bottom of the bowl that aren't cooperating, you can sprinkle an extra teaspoon or two (5 to 10 ml) of buttermilk over those bits. Gather the dough into a ball, and place it on a floured counter. Roll or pat the dough out with a floured rolling pin or your hands, until it's between ½ and ¾ inch (1.3 and 2 cm) thick.

Dip a biscuit cutter (mine is 3 inches [8 cm] across) or a similar-sized drinking glass into flour and cut out four to five biscuits, flouring the cutter between each use. Don't twist the cutter when you cut the biscuits—this can seal off the edges and prevent them from rising. Gather the scraps and flour your counter and flour the dough again if it's sticky. Pat it out and cut one to two more biscuits. You should have six to seven biscuits total.

(continued)

EVERYTHING BUT THE KITCHEN SINK MIXED BERRY
Cobbler (CONT.)

FOR THE BISCUITS AND FOR SERVING

2 cups (280 g) all-purpose flour, plus more as needed

2 tsp (8 g) baking powder

½ tsp salt

⅛ tsp cinnamon

¼ cup (53 g) granulated sugar

½ cup (1 stick or 113 g) cold salted butter

⅔ cup (160 ml) buttermilk, plus 1 tsp if needed

1–2 tbsp (15–30 ml) heavy cream

Generous sprinkle of coarse or raw sugar

Vanilla ice cream or 1 batch Classic Vanilla Whipped Cream (page 158)

Stir the fruit filling, and make sure it's evenly spread out so the biscuits will lay flat on top. Place the biscuits on top of the filling, and pop in the fridge for 5 minutes to chill.

BAKE: Brush the tops of the biscuits with a little heavy cream, and sprinkle with coarse or raw sugar. Bake for 48 to 50 minutes. The biscuits will be golden brown, and the filling should be bubbly all the way through.

SERVE AND STORE: Let the cobbler rest about 10 minutes before serving. Serve plain or with Classic Vanilla Whipped Cream (page 158) or vanilla ice cream. Store leftovers, covered, in the fridge for 3 to 4 days.

> *Tip* You can use milk and lemon juice to sub for buttermilk if you'd like. Just add 2 tsp (10 ml) of lemon juice to your glass measuring cup, and then add milk until you hit the ⅔-cup (160-ml) line. Stir and let it sit for 5 minutes before using. Voilà—homemade buttermilk!

CARAMEL PEACH *Pandowdy*

Don't be scared by the name "pandowdy." It's just a fancy way of saying that this recipe uses puff pastry as the topping. This dessert is like a peach cobbler, but it's even easier to create thanks to a topping made from store-bought puff pastry. The caramel peach filling is incredible paired with the crisp, golden-brown, cinnamon-sugar-studded pastry on top!

Yield: 4–6 SERVINGS

FOR THE FILLING

6 large or 8 medium peaches (about 2 lb or 907 g), sliced between ¼" and ½" (6 and 13 mm) thick

2 tbsp (16 g) cornstarch

⅓ cup (80 g) packed brown sugar

¾ tsp cinnamon

1 tsp vanilla extract

1 tsp lemon juice

½ cup (120 ml) 10-Minute Salted Caramel Sauce (page 150)

FOR THE TOPPING AND FOR SERVING

1 sheet frozen puff pastry, thawed according to package directions

All-purpose flour, for dusting

1 egg, for egg wash

Cinnamon sugar and raw sugar, for sprinkling

Vanilla ice cream or 1 batch Classic Vanilla Whipped Cream (page 158), for serving

PREP: Preheat the oven to 400°F (200°C).

MAKE THE FILLING: Add the peach slices to a 10-inch (25-cm) oven-safe skillet or baking dish. Stir in the cornstarch, brown sugar, cinnamon, vanilla and lemon juice. Once the filling is all mixed together, pour the 10-Minute Salted Caramel Sauce (page 150) over the filling and toss to combine.

MAKE THE TOPPING: Roll the thawed, but still cold, sheet of puff pastry out on a lightly floured counter. I rolled mine to about 12 x 10 inches (30 x 25 cm). Use cookie cutters or even the rim of a small drinking glass or shot glass to cut out circles or other shapes. I used star cookie cutters to give this a fun flair. Place the pieces of puff pastry all over the top of the peach filling. It's fine if they overlap. Beat the egg with a fork in the dirtied measuring cup, and brush it over the top of all the puff pastry pieces. Sprinkle some cinnamon sugar and a bit of raw sugar over the top of the puff pastry. (If you're going to just do one type of sugar, it needs to be the cinnamon sugar—so good!)

BAKE: Bake for 35 to 41 minutes. The filling will be very bubbly, and the puff pastry should be a deep golden brown.

SERVE AND STORE: Let it rest for about 10 minutes before serving. Enjoy while it's warm with vanilla ice cream or Classic Vanilla Whipped Cream (page 158). This is absolutely best fresh from the oven, but leftovers can be stored tightly covered in the fridge for 2 to 3 days.

DOUBLE CHOCOLATE *Cobbler*

Have you ever had a chocolate lava cake? This Chocolate Cobbler is essentially one huge chocolate lava cake baked in a skillet. When you scoop a serving out, you'll find a river of molten chocolate underneath the fluffy chocolate cobbler on top. Sheer perfection—especially served piping hot with a scoop of vanilla ice cream.

Yield: **4–6 SERVINGS**

FOR THE CHOCOLATE COBBLER

6 tbsp (85 g) salted butter

½ cup (120 ml) milk

1½ tsp (8 ml) vanilla extract

¼ cup (60 g) packed brown sugar

½ cup (105 g) granulated sugar

¼ tsp salt

1 tsp espresso powder

1 cup (140 g) all-purpose flour

2 tsp (8 g) baking powder

¼ cup (25 g) cocoa powder

¾ cup (146 g) chocolate chips

FOR THE TOPPING AND FOR SERVING

1 cup (240 g) packed brown sugar

3 tbsp (19 g) cocoa powder

1½ cups (360 ml) very hot water

Vanilla ice cream or 1 batch Classic Vanilla Whipped Cream (page 158)

PREP: Preheat the oven to 350°F (180°C). Spray a 10-inch (25-cm) oven-safe skillet or baking dish with nonstick spray.

MAKE THE CHOCOLATE COBBLER: Melt the butter in a large mixing bowl in the microwave. Whisk in the milk and vanilla. Whisk in the brown sugar and granulated sugar. Add the salt, espresso powder, flour, baking powder, cocoa powder and chocolate chips, and whisk until everything is well combined, scraping the sides of the bowl as needed. It'll look like a smooth brownie batter. Spread the batter into the prepared skillet.

ADD THE TOPPING: Sprinkle the brown sugar and then the cocoa powder on top of the batter. Pour the hot water over the top of this. Don't stir any of these ingredients into the batter.

BAKE: Bake for 38 to 40 minutes. The cobbler will be bubbly and a little crinkly around the edges (like a pan of brownies), and it will have a slight jiggle when you move the pan. A toothpick inserted in the cobbler will come out clean or with a few moist crumbs. Let it sit for 10 to 20 minutes before serving so it can set up a bit.

SERVE AND STORE: Serve warm with vanilla ice cream or Classic Vanilla Whipped Cream (page 158). Store leftovers, covered, at room temperature for 2 to 3 days.

STRAWBERRY RHUBARB *Crisp*

I excitedly await the arrival of rhubarb season each spring. It's one of my favorite seasonal things to bake with. Tart rhubarb is absolutely heavenly paired with fresh, sweet strawberries and nestled under a perfectly golden-brown, crisp brown sugar topping. You'll want to make this every day of rhubarb season. And, if you're like me, you'll start stashing rhubarb in your freezer so you can have this any time of year.

Yield: 4-6 SERVINGS

FOR THE FILLING

⅔ cup plus 3 tbsp (179 g) granulated sugar

⅓ cup (45 g) all-purpose flour

2 cups (248 g) rinsed, dried and chopped rhubarb (1–2" [2.5–5-cm] pieces)

2⅔ cups (390 g) rinsed, hulled and halved (or quartered if they're quite large) strawberries

2 tsp (10 ml) lemon juice

1 tsp vanilla extract

¼ tsp cinnamon

FOR THE TOPPING AND FOR SERVING

½ cup plus 1 tbsp (80 g) all-purpose flour

¾ cup (180 g) packed brown sugar

½ tsp cinnamon

¼ tsp salt

½ cup (1 stick or 113 g) plus 1 tbsp (14 g) cold salted butter

1 cup (100 g) old-fashioned whole rolled oats

Vanilla ice cream or 1 batch Classic Vanilla Whipped Cream (page 158)

PREP: Preheat the oven to 350°F (180°C).

MAKE THE FILLING: Add the sugar and flour to a 9-inch (23-cm) baking dish or pie plate, and whisk together well. Add the rhubarb, strawberries, lemon juice, vanilla and cinnamon, and stir everything together well. Make sure to get in under the fruit so there aren't any clumps of dry flour and sugar hiding underneath.

MAKE THE TOPPING: In a medium mixing bowl, whisk together the flour, brown sugar, cinnamon and salt. Cut the cold butter into tablespoon-sized (14-g) cubes. Cut the butter into the dry ingredients using a pastry cutter or clean hands, until you have a mix of blueberry-sized chunks scattered throughout the flour mixture. Stir in the oats.

Give the filling in the baking dish one more stir. Sprinkle the topping evenly over the filling.

BAKE: Bake for 45 minutes. The filling will be very bubbly around the edges, and the topping will be golden brown and crisp. Let it rest for 10 minutes before serving.

SERVE AND STORE: Enjoy this while it's nice and warm from the oven, preferably with vanilla ice cream or Classic Vanilla Whipped Cream (page 158). This is at its very best while it's fresh, but leftovers can be covered and stored in the fridge for 2 to 3 days.

BLUEBERRY *Cobbler for Two*

This is the perfect summertime dessert! Juicy blueberries mingle with vanilla and a hint of lemon, underneath a topping of fluffy, lightly sweetened biscuits. The biscuits are easy to make—and so is the cobbler, since we're just stirring the fruit filling together right in the baking dish. Some call it lazy. I call it brilliant. Promise to enjoy this warm, with vanilla ice cream.

Yield: **2 GENEROUS SERVINGS**

FOR THE FILLING

2 tbsp (18 g) all-purpose flour

⅓ cup (70 g) granulated sugar

2 tbsp (26 g) packed brown sugar

2½ cups (345 g) fresh or frozen blueberries (if using frozen, don't thaw them)

1 tbsp (15 ml) lemon juice

1 tsp lemon zest

1 tsp vanilla extract

¼ tsp cinnamon

FOR THE TOPPING AND FOR SERVING

1 cup (140 g) all-purpose flour, plus more as needed

3 tbsp (40 g) granulated sugar

1 tbsp (13 g) packed brown sugar

1 tsp baking powder

½ tsp salt

¼ tsp cinnamon

¼ cup (½ stick or 57 g) cold salted butter

5 tbsp (75 ml) cold milk, plus a splash extra if needed

About ½ tbsp (8 ml) heavy cream

Generous sprinkle of raw or coarse sugar

Vanilla ice cream or 1 batch Classic Vanilla Whipped Cream (page 158)

PREP: Preheat the oven to 375°F (190°C). Get out a 6-inch (15-cm) baking dish.

MAKE THE FILLING: Whisk together the flour, granulated sugar and brown sugar in the baking dish. Add the blueberries, lemon juice, lemon zest, vanilla and cinnamon, and stir well to get all the ingredients combined. Make sure to get under the fruit so that there aren't any big clumps of flour or sugar left. Set aside while you make the topping.

MAKE THE TOPPING: In a medium mixing bowl, whisk together the flour, granulated sugar, brown sugar, baking powder, salt and cinnamon. Cut the cold butter into tablespoon-sized (14-g) chunks (does not need to be perfect), and add them to the bowl. Cut the butter into the dry ingredients using a pastry cutter or clean hands, until you have chunks the size of walnut halves. Stir in the milk. Gently gather the dough into a ball in the bowl, and flick a little bit of extra milk on any dry bits left in the bottom of the bowl, so you can gather them into the rest of the dough.

Lightly flour your counter, and gently flatten the dough out so it's about ½ to ¾ inch (1.3 to 2 cm) thick. Use a biscuit cutter (mine was 3 inches [8 cm]) or a glass to cut out two biscuits. Don't twist the cutter as this can seal the edges, preventing the biscuits from rising. Gently gather the scraps together and press back out to the same thickness, so you can cut one more biscuit.

Give the filling in the dish one more stir, and make sure it's in an even layer so the biscuits will lay nicely on top. Place the three biscuits on top of the filling. Brush them with the heavy cream and sprinkle with a little coarse sugar.

BAKE: Bake for 45 to 48 minutes. The filling will be juicy and very bubbly, and the biscuits will be golden brown.

SERVE AND STORE: Let the cobbler rest about 10 minutes before digging in. Enjoy with vanilla ice cream, Classic Vanilla Whipped Cream (page 158) or even plain. Store leftovers, tightly covered, in the fridge for 2 to 3 days.

BREAKFAST *and* BRUNCH BITES

I'm a firm believer that there's absolutely nothing like a warm, homemade breakfast—especially on a crisp fall morning. The feeling of stirring up batter for banana or pumpkin bread, the sound of eggs cracking against the side of your most well-loved mixing bowl and, of course, the intoxicating aromas that waft from your oven as you anxiously await that first bite of a fresh-baked cinnamon roll. Now I'm starving for some breakfast bakes—aren't you?

This chapter covers a little bit of everything—muffins, scones, biscuits, quick breads and even a few unexpected treats: Monkey Bread Muffins (page 131), Rich Chocolate Granola (page 132) and Zingy Homemade Cherry Pop Tarts (page 119). The recipes in this chapter range from lickety-split (Muffins! Quick breads!) to things that take a little more love and time (Overnight cinnamon rolls! Homemade pop tarts!). But they're still all easy enough for you to pull off, no matter the occasion. No need to get out two bowls to make your quick breads, scones and biscuits—I've eliminated the step where you measure out dry ingredients in one bowl and wet ingredients in another. It can all be done in just one bowl. And I've come up with a few little cheats to even help keep something like cinnamon rolls in the one-bowl baking game.

Whatever your brunch fancy is, you're sure to find something in this chapter that you'll turn to again and again for every breakfast craving.

MAPLE CINNAMON *Biscuits*

I love adding cinnamon and maple to anything and everything I possibly can. It's a flavor combination made in heaven. These biscuits are crispy on top, flaky and tender the rest of the way down and taste like a fall explosion in your mouth. Although biscuits might scream "tons of dishes!", these really are made in just one bowl—and don't be intimidated by a longer set of directions. I wanted to be thorough to ensure you can make delicious biscuits at home.

Yield: **7–8 BISCUITS**

FOR THE DOUGH

2¾ cups (385 g) all-purpose flour, plus more as needed

3 tbsp (40 g) granulated sugar

1 tbsp plus 1 tsp (16 g) baking powder

½ tsp baking soda

1½ tsp (9 g) salt

1 tbsp (8 g) cinnamon

¾ cup (1½ sticks or 170 g) plus 2 tbsp (28 g) cold salted butter

1 egg

⅔ cup (160 ml) milk

¼ cup (60 ml) real maple syrup

1 tsp vanilla extract

MAKE THE DOUGH: In a large mixing bowl, whisk together the flour, sugar, baking powder, baking soda, salt and cinnamon. Cut the cold butter into tablespoon-sized (14-g) cubes and add to the dry ingredients. Cut the butter in with a pastry cutter or clean hands until you have pieces about the size of walnut halves. Beat the egg in the same measuring glass as you'll use for the milk, and pour it into the bowl. Add the milk, maple syrup and vanilla to the bowl. Stir everything together, making sure to get the dry bits hiding at the bottom. Cover the bowl and chill in the fridge for 30 minutes.

After the 30 minutes are up, flour your counter and dump the dough out. It will be fairly moist—sprinkle it lightly with flour. Before you begin the process outlined below, I recommend writing #1, #2, #3 and #4 on a scrap piece of paper so you can keep track of the 4 times you have to roll out and fold the dough. Cross each number off as you pass it, so you don't lose track.

With floured hands, gently pat the dough into a rectangle about ¾ inch (2 cm) thick and about two times longer than it is wide, pushing any stray pieces into place as best you can. It does not need to be perfect. With the long side perpendicular to you, fold each side in thirds like a letter. Flip the dough over, flour your rolling pin and gently roll back into a rectangle that's about ½ inch (1.3 cm) thick and is similar in size again—about two times longer than it is wide. Flour underneath and on the dough again as needed. (It will likely try to stick to your counter a bit between each turn.) Repeat this process three more times, for a total of four times, but, on the fourth time, roll it back to ¾-inch (2-cm) thickness again.

Chill the dough on a baking sheet, covered with a kitchen towel, for 30 minutes.

PREP: Preheat the oven to 400°F (200°C). Line a baking sheet with parchment paper or a silicone baking mat.

(continued)

MAPLE CINNAMON *Biscuits* (CONT.)

FOR THE TOPPING

1 tsp cinnamon

2 tbsp (26 g) granulated sugar

1–2 tbsp (15–30 ml) heavy cream, for brushing on top of scones

FOR THE BUTTERY MAPLE GLAZE

1 batch Infinitely Adaptable Glaze (page 157)

¼ cup (½ stick or 57 g) salted butter

2 tbsp (30 ml) maple syrup

MAKE THE TOPPING: Stir together the cinnamon and sugar in a used measuring cup.

CUT OUT THE BISCUITS AND BAKE: Cut out biscuits using a 3-inch (8-cm) biscuit cutter, flouring it between each use to prevent sticking. Do NOT twist the cutter. This can seal off the edges, preventing the biscuits from rising as well. Once you get five to six biscuits from the initial piece of dough, gently smush the scraps back together and cut out one to two more. (You may have to push the scraps together two times to cut out two more.) Place the biscuits on the prepared baking sheet, brush the tops with a light layer of heavy cream and sprinkle with the cinnamon sugar. It will seem like a lot of cinnamon sugar, but use all of it.

Bake for 17 minutes. If any of your biscuits are larger (my scrap piece biscuits sometimes were), they might need an extra 1 to 3 minutes. You will be able to see patches of wet dough on the top if they aren't done. You can also gently lift the biscuit open from the side with a butter knife to check the doneness inside. You shouldn't see any wet dough spots. Let them cool a few minutes before topping with the glaze. You MUST enjoy these while they're nice and warm. They're absolutely the best on the first day and will only be crisp on the first day, but leftovers can be stored in an airtight container at room temperature for an extra day or two.

MAKE THE GLAZE: While the biscuits bake, make the glaze. Follow the directions for my Infinitely Adaptable Glaze (page 157), but start by melting the butter in a small bowl or glass measuring cup. Whisk in the remaining ingredients, including the maple syrup, and pour this over your hot biscuits.

CARAMELIZED WHITE CHOCOLATE PEACH *Scones*

When peaches are in season, I consider it my moral duty to squeeze them into each and every recipe I possibly can. They're a little tricky to get into scones—blotting out excess moisture is super important so the scones don't turn into a puddle in your oven. But, that smidgen of extra work is absolutely worth it, as these scones are crisp on top, tender inside and the flavors of fresh peaches, cinnamon sugar and caramelized white chocolate dance together wonderfully.

Yield: **8 SCONES**

FOR THE SCONES

6 oz (170 g) white chocolate, roughly chopped

1½ cups (240 g or about 2 medium) fresh peaches

2 cups plus 2 tbsp (298 g) all-purpose flour, divided

¾ cup (158 g) granulated sugar

½ tsp salt

1 tbsp (12 g) baking powder

1¼ tsp (4 g) cinnamon

¼ cup (60 ml) milk

1 large egg

1 tsp vanilla extract

½ cup (1 stick or 113 g) cold salted butter, cubed

MAKE THE CARAMELIZED WHITE CHOCOLATE: Preheat the oven to 255°F (125°C). Place the chopped white chocolate in an even layer on a nonstick baking sheet. Melt the chocolate in the oven for 10 minutes. Use an offset spatula or a silicone spatula to stir and spread the chocolate evenly on the pan. Don't worry if it's a little grainy or lumpy—it'll smooth out as you continue roasting and spreading it. Put the sheet back in the oven, and continue roasting the chocolate for three intervals of 10 minutes (for a total of 40 minutes), scraping up the chocolate and smoothing it back out onto an even layer on the pan between each interval. It should be a golden toffee color at the end. When it's done, pop the pan in the fridge to cool so that you can break the chocolate into shards. The caramelized white chocolate can be made ahead of time and stored in the fridge in an airtight container or mason jar for up to 2 weeks.

MAKE THE SCONES: Line a baking sheet with parchment paper or a silicone baking mat.

Cut the peaches into bite-sized chunks. Shake off any excess liquid from the cutting board you cut the peaches on, and then spread the peach pieces into an even layer. Place a paper towel over them and press them gently but firmly—we're just trying to remove excess liquid, not smush them into oblivion. Once that paper towel is all wet, repeat with another clean paper towel until excess moisture is gone. Sprinkle 2 tablespoons (18 g) of the flour over the blotted peaches and toss to coat them. Let them rest on the cutting board while you finish mixing up the scones.

In a large mixing bowl, whisk together the remaining flour, sugar, salt, baking powder and cinnamon. Measure the milk into a glass measuring cup, add the egg and vanilla and beat with a fork to break up the egg and mix the ingredients together. Pop this in the fridge. Cut the cold butter into tablespoon-sized (14-g) cubes and add to the dry ingredients. Cut the butter into the dry ingredients using a pastry cutter or clean hands until you have chunks of butter about the size of blueberries. Stir in the peaches and the caramelized white chocolate shards.

(continued)

CARAMELIZED WHITE CHOCOLATE
PEACH *Scones* (CONT.)

**FOR THE TOPPING AND
FOR SERVING**

¼ tsp cinnamon

1¼ tsp (6 g) granulated sugar

1–2 tbsp (15–30 ml) cold
heavy cream

1 batch Infinitely Adaptable Glaze
(page 157; optional)

Butter, for slathering (optional)

Pour the wet ingredients into the dry ingredients, and stir everything together gently with a wooden spoon, making sure to get any dry bits hiding at the bottom of the bowl, until you have a dough. Gently form this into a ball on your prepared pan, and flatten into a disk that's 8 inches (20 cm) in diameter. Slice the disk into eight slices. Cover the pan with a clean kitchen towel, and chill in the fridge for 20 minutes.

Preheat the oven to 400°F (200°C).

MAKE THE TOPPING: In a dirtied measuring cup, mix together the cinnamon and sugar.

BAKE: Once the scones have chilled, brush the tops with a light layer of heavy cream, and sprinkle with cinnamon sugar. Bake for 10 minutes. Then turn the oven down to 350°F (180°C). Bake for 25 minutes. Remove the pan from the oven, and use a knife to gently nudge the scones apart so there's some space between them. This allows the edges to fully cook. Return the pan to the oven and bake for 10 to 11 minutes. The tops should be a bit crisp and the sides shouldn't seem wet.

SERVE AND STORE: If desired, top with 1 batch of Infinitely Adaptable Glaze (page 157). Drizzle over the scones while they're still warm, and enjoy immediately. You can also enjoy them plain or with a slather of butter. These are best on the first day, but cooled scones can be stored in an airtight container at room temperature for 2 to 3 days.

ANY FRUIT *Muffins*

These classic muffins are soft and moist, and are a breeze to whip up. Serve them with eggs and juice for an easy brunch, or as grab-and-go-breakfasts throughout your week. They work well with any type of berries, but I love using strawberries and blueberries in mine.

Yield: **12–13 MUFFINS**

6 tbsp (85 g) salted butter

⅔ cup (139 g) granulated sugar

1 tsp lemon zest

¾ cup (180 ml) buttermilk

1 large egg

1⅔ cups (234 g) all-purpose flour

½ tsp cinnamon

¼ tsp nutmeg

¼ tsp salt

¼ tsp baking soda

1½ tsp (7 g) baking powder

2 cups (250 g) berries (blueberries, quartered strawberries, blackberries, raspberries, etc.)

Generous sprinkle of raw sugar, for topping

1 batch Infinitely Adaptable Glaze (page 157), for serving (optional)

PREP: Preheat the oven to 375°F (190°C). Line a muffin tin with muffin liners.

MAKE THE MUFFINS: Melt the butter in a large mixing bowl in the microwave. Whisk in the sugar, lemon zest and buttermilk. The mixture won't look smooth—it'll have some lumps, but that's okay! Whisk in the egg. Add the flour, cinnamon, nutmeg, salt, baking soda and baking powder, and stir until just combined, scraping the bowl as needed. The batter should be smooth now. Stir in the fruit. (I sometimes divide the batter and use strawberries in one half and blueberries in the other.)

BAKE: Spoon the batter into the muffin tins until they're about two-thirds full. Sprinkle a little raw sugar over the top of the muffin batter. Bake for 18 to 20 minutes. A toothpick inserted in the center should be clean or have a few moist crumbs on it. Top with 1 batch of my Infinitely Adaptable Glaze (page 157), if desired, or enjoy with a slather of butter.

SERVE AND STORE: Enjoy right away! Store leftovers in an airtight container at room temperature for 1 to 2 days, or in the fridge for 3 to 4 days.

> *Tip* You can use regular milk instead of buttermilk. Just add 2 teaspoons (10 ml) of lemon juice to your glass measuring cup, and then add milk until you hit the ¾-cup (180-ml) line. Stir and let sit for 5 minutes before using. Voilà—homemade buttermilk.

MAPLE BACON *Cinnamon Rolls*

You know how the soft center of a cinnamon roll is universally accepted as the best part? Well, everyone who's had these cinnamon rolls tells me that the whole roll is like the center part of a normal roll. The secret is using an overnight brioche dough sweetened with maple syrup. The overnight dough makes these a bit easier to make than traditional cinnamon rolls—the work is broken up into simple steps, and the dough is very forgiving. There's maple syrup and bacon in the filling as well as the frosting, so you know these treats are going to be reeeeal good.

Yield: **9–11 ROLLS**

FOR THE DOUGH

6 tbsp (85 g) salted butter

1 tsp instant yeast

½ tsp salt

3 tbsp (45 ml) pure maple syrup

½ cup (120 ml) lukewarm water

2 large eggs, at room temperature

2¼ cups (315 g) all-purpose flour, plus more as needed

FOR THE FILLING

½ cup (1 stick or 113 g) salted butter, softened

½ cup (105 g) granulated sugar

¼ cup (60 g) packed brown sugar

1 tbsp (8 g) cinnamon

¼ tsp nutmeg

2 tbsp (30 ml) pure maple syrup

10 slices cooked bacon, broken into small pieces

MAKE THE DOUGH: In a medium mixing bowl, melt the butter. Whisk in the yeast, salt, maple syrup, water and eggs, and then stir in the flour. The dough will be sticky and shaggy. Cover loosely with plastic wrap or a kitchen towel and let rest for 2 hours in a warm place.

After 2 hours, cover the bowl tightly with plastic wrap and refrigerate overnight (about 10 hours). My ideal schedule for these cinnamon rolls is mixing up the dough around 8:00 p.m., moving it to the fridge around 10:00 p.m. and preparing and baking the cinnamon rolls at 8:00 or 9:00 a.m. the next morning.

PREPARE THE CINNAMON ROLLS: The next morning, sprinkle a generous dusting of flour over your counter to prevent sticking. Dump the dough onto the floured counter, scraping any stray bits from the bowl with a spatula, and lightly flour the top of the dough. Gently shape it into a large, thick rectangle shape.

Flour your rolling pin, and begin rolling out the dough. We're going for a long rectangle that's about 18 x 12 inches (46 x 30 cm).

MAKE THE FILLING: Spread the softened butter over the rolled-out dough, using a silicone spatula to avoid tearing the dough. Using the same bowl the dough was in, stir together the granulated sugar, brown sugar, cinnamon and nutmeg, and sprinkle this evenly over the butter. Drizzle the maple syrup over the filling, and then scatter the bacon pieces over the dough.

Slowly roll the dough into a log, rolling from the long side. Go slow here, and make sure you're rolling tightly. Run an offset spatula gently under any parts of the dough that are sticking a bit to the counter. If you get a few small tears in the dough, that's fine.

Use a piece of string, a sharp serrated knife or unflavored dental floss to cut your cinnamon rolls into slices that are about 2¼ inches (6 cm) wide. Spray a 9-inch (23-cm) round baking dish or pie dish with nonstick spray. Place the pieces cut side up in the prepared dish and cover loosely with a kitchen towel. Let them rise for 30 minutes. Preheat the oven to 350°F (180°C).

(continued)

MAPLE BACON *Cinnamon Rolls* (CONT.)

FOR THE MAPLE FROSTING

¼ cup (½ stick or 57 g) salted butter, softened at room temperature

6 oz (170 g) cream cheese, softened at room temperature

1½ cups (180 g) powdered sugar

1 tsp vanilla

3 tbsp (45 ml) real maple syrup

¼ tsp maple extract

1 tbsp (15 ml) milk (optional)

6–8 slices cooked bacon, broken into small pieces

BAKE: Once the cinnamon rolls have risen, bake for 30 to 32 minutes, or until a cooking thermometer inserted into the center of one of the rolls registers about 185°F (85°C). The cinnamon rolls should be golden brown and shouldn't seem too doughy if you poke into the center of one with a knife.

MAKE THE FROSTING: While the cinnamon rolls bake, mix up the frosting. Use the same bowl that you mixed the filling up in—just give it a quick rinse and wipe with a kitchen towel. Beat the softened butter and cream cheese with an electric mixer on high speed until nice and creamy. Add the powdered sugar, and mix until combined (start on low speed so powder doesn't fly everywhere). Add the vanilla, maple syrup and maple extract, and mix until just combined. Add the milk if you want to thin the frosting out a tad more. Stir in the bacon pieces.

SERVE AND STORE: Spread the frosting over the warm cinnamon rolls and dig in. Store leftovers, covered, in the fridge for up to 4 days. Microwave to reheat. These are best served fresh from the oven, however.

Tip If you forgot to let the butter for the cinnamon roll filling soften to room temperature, pop it on a plate, and microwave it for about 15 to 20 seconds just to soften it but not melt it. (If it gets a little melty, that's fine.)

ZINGY HOMEMADE CHERRY
Pop Tarts

I didn't really get to eat store-bought pop tarts growing up, but every time we visited my grandparents in Montana, they had a box waiting for me. If you loved (and still love) pop tarts, be prepared to have your mind blown by the homemade version. The crust is 100x more buttery and flaky, and the filling and glaze are dead simple. The cherry flavor in these is incredible—it's sweet with a hint of zingy tartness!

Yield: 12 POP TARTS

FOR THE CRUST

1 cup (140 g) white whole-wheat flour (or sub with all-purpose flour in a pinch), plus more as needed

2 cups (280 g) all-purpose flour

¾ tsp salt

1 cup (2 sticks or 226 g) plus 2 tbsp (28 g) cold salted butter

10–11 tbsp (150–165 ml) cold water, or more as needed

1 egg

FOR THE FILLING

1½ (13-oz [370-g]) jars cherry preserves (I like Bonne Maman's preserves)

Zest of 2 oranges, divided

FOR THE GLAZE

1 batch Infinitely Adaptable Glaze (page 157)

2 tbsp (40 g) cherry preserves

1 tbsp (15 ml) milk, plus a splash

Orange zest, for topping

MAKE THE DOUGH: In a medium mixing bowl, whisk together the whole-wheat flour, all-purpose flour and salt. Cut the cold butter into tablespoon-sized (14-g) cubes, and add to the dry ingredients. Use a pastry cutter or clean hands to cut the butter into the dry ingredients until you have chunks the size of walnut halves. (Some will be a bit bigger and some a bit smaller.) Drizzle in 5 tablespoons (75 ml) of the cold water. Toss with a fork to mix this in, and then repeat with the remaining water. If you can gather the dough into a ball and it holds, it's ready. If it still seems pretty dry, add more water, a tablespoon (15 ml) at a time, until it holds together when you form a ball. The dough shouldn't be sticky or wet, though.

Gently gather the dough into a ball. If there are still a few small dry areas, flick some water onto the dry bits. (There are usually some dry bits hiding in the bottom of the bowl.) Slice the dough ball in half with a knife and gently reform into two balls. Gently flatten each ball into a 1-inch (2.5-cm)-thick disk. Push any crumbly bits into place as best you can, and try to make sure there isn't a fissure in the disks that is causing them to fall apart. The dough discs may look a little scrappy, but they should hold together.

Wrap each disk tightly in plastic wrap, and chill in the freezer for at least 1 hour or in the fridge for at least 2 hours and up to 3 days. The dough can also be frozen for up to 2 months—let it thaw in the fridge overnight before using. If you freeze the dough for 1 hour, and your filling isn't ready yet, move the dough to the fridge so it doesn't freeze solid on you.

ASSEMBLE THE POP TARTS: Line a few baking sheets with parchment paper or silicone baking mats. Beat the egg in a used measuring cup—this is your egg wash. Keep it in the fridge until ready to use.

Once the dough has chilled, flour your counter and rolling pin. Get out one dough disk—leave the other in the fridge for now. I like to work with one at a time, and once the first baking sheet of pop tarts is in the oven, I start the process over with the next disk.

(continued)

Unwrap the dough and sprinkle a little flour on top. Starting in the center of the disk, gently roll the dough out in all directions. Turn the dough every few rolls to make sure it's not sticking to the counter—lightly re-flour the counter if it is sticking, and sprinkle a little more flour on the dough. Push together any cracked areas and continue rolling. Roll the dough out to about 14 to 16 inches (35 to 41 cm) and about ⅛ inch (3 mm) thick. (I've done it at 14 x 14 inches [35 x 35 cm] and 16 x 13 inches [41 x 33 cm]. It doesn't have to be perfect.)

Cut rectangles that are about 3 x 4½ inches (8 x 11 cm). A ruler is useful here. You should have eight rectangles. Gently gather the scraps together into a ball. Wrap them back up in the plastic wrap and pop in the fridge to re-chill a bit while you assemble the first round of pop tarts. Arrange half of the rectangles on your prepared baking sheets. These are your bottom crusts. Brush the outer edges, all the way around, with the egg wash.

Place about 1½ tablespoons (30 g) of cherry preserves in the center of each rectangle, and sprinkle on a pinch of orange zest. Place a top crust over the filling. Use your fingertip to seal the top crust to the bottom crust by pressing the top edge into the bottom edge. It's okay if some filling leaks out.

Cover the baking sheet with a kitchen towel, and pop it in the fridge for 15 minutes or in the freezer for 10 minutes. This will help re-chill the dough before baking, since we've been handling it. Crimp the edges of the chilled pop tarts with the tines of a fork. Prick an "X" in the top of each pop tart with the fork.

Preheat your oven to 375°F (190°C).

While the first pan of pop tarts chills, take out the second dough disk and repeat everything again, pausing if needed to put the first pan of pop tarts in the oven. Combine these dough scraps with the other dough scraps, wrap and pop back in the fridge.

BAKE: Brush the tops of each pop tart with egg wash. Bake for 28 minutes. (Meanwhile, your second pan should be chilling.) The pop tarts will be golden brown and crisp. While the first pan of pop tarts bakes, roll the dough remnant piece back out (re-flour your counter and rolling pin). Mine was about 12 x 12 inches (30 x 30 cm). Cut as many rectangles out as you can, and repeat the steps above to bake the second and third pans of pop tarts. At this point, the remaining scraps aren't worth re-rolling again. See page 76 for a tip on making pie crust chips with the remaining dough scraps.

MAKE THE GLAZE: In a small bowl combine the Infinitely Adaptable Glaze (page 157), cherry preserves and milk.

SERVE AND STORE: Let the pop tarts cool on the baking sheet while you mix up the glaze. Spoon the glaze over them once they're cool enough to handle, and sprinkle a little orange zest on top of each pop tart. These are best fresh but can be stored in an airtight container in the fridge for 2 to 3 days.

Tips *If you chilled your dough longer than the minimum time, you may need to let it sit for a few minutes at room temperature before rolling it out. If it's cracking a lot as you try to roll it, this is why. I find that I don't have to do this often, but I sometimes do during colder months.*

Assembled pop tarts can be frozen, without the egg wash, on a baking sheet and then transferred to a freezer-safe container (so they don't stick together). Bake up a few pop tarts whenever you want! Simply bake them from frozen, following the rest of the directions as written.

SMALL-BATCH GINGERBREAD *Scones*

Gingerbread is my all-time favorite flavor. It's warm and cozy, and full of SO many spices! Drizzle some buttery maple glaze on top as soon as these beauties are out of the oven, and you are in business.

Yield: **4 SCONES**

FOR THE SCONES

1 cup (140 g) all-purpose flour

3 tbsp (39 g) packed brown sugar

¼ tsp salt

1½ tsp (7 g) baking powder

¾ tsp ground ginger

½ plus ⅛ tsp cinnamon

⅛ tsp ground nutmeg

Pinch of ground cloves

¼ cup (60 ml) molasses

1 tbsp (15 ml) milk, plus extra for topping

¼ tsp vanilla extract

½ egg

3 tbsp (42 g) cold salted butter

Generous sprinkle of raw sugar, for topping

FOR THE BUTTER MAPLE GLAZE

½ batch Infinitely Adaptable Glaze (page 157)

2 tbsp (28 g) salted butter

1 tbsp (15 ml) real maple syrup

Pinch of cinnamon

Pinch of ground ginger

Splash of molasses (if you want an even more intense gingerbread flavor)

Splash of milk, as needed

PREP: Line a small baking sheet with parchment paper. Preheat the oven to 400°F (200°C).

MAKE THE SCONES: In a medium mixing bowl, whisk together the flour, brown sugar, salt, baking powder, ginger, cinnamon, nutmeg and cloves. Measure the molasses into a 1-cup (240-ml) glass measuring cup. Add the milk and vanilla to the measuring cup with the molasses. Crack the egg into another dirtied measuring cup. Beat the egg well with a fork, and measure 2 tablespoons (30 ml) into the glass measuring cup with the wet ingredients. (Save the remaining egg for another small-batch recipe.) Whisk the liquid ingredients in the measuring cup, and pop it into the fridge.

Slice the butter into three cubes, and add to the dry ingredients. Cut in the butter using a pastry cutter or clean hands until you have pieces of butter the size of blueberries. (Some will be a bit larger, some smaller.) Add the wet ingredients that were mixed earlier, and stir everything together to form a dough. Gently shape the dough into a ball, and transfer it to the prepared baking sheet. Gently press it into a disk that's about 5 x 6 inches (13 x 15 cm) across and ½ inch (1.3 cm) thick. If it's a bit sticky, lightly flour your hands to do this. Spray a little nonstick spray on your knife to make clean cuts, and cut the disk into four pieces.

Pop a clean kitchen towel over the scones and chill in the fridge for 15 minutes.

BAKE: Once the scones have chilled, brush the tops with a little milk, and sprinkle with a little raw or coarse sugar. Bake for 10 minutes. Turn the oven down to 350°F (180°C). Bake for 12 minutes, and then remove the pan from the oven. Gently nudge the scones apart with a knife so the edges can finish cooking. Bake for 5 more minutes.

MAKE THE GLAZE: Make the Infinitely Adaptable Glaze (page 157) while the scones finish baking, but start by melting the butter in a small bowl. Then, whisk in the maple syrup, cinnamon, ginger, molasses (if using) and milk (if using).

SERVE AND STORE: Drizzle the glaze over the scones while they're fresh out of the oven, and enjoy immediately. These are best while warm from the oven. I don't really recommend keeping leftovers for this recipe—just enjoy them while they're hot.

CHAI-SPICED *Pumpkin Bread*

I have to thank my mom for my pumpkin bread obsession. She bakes it often, and she bakes it well! This loaf is a classic pumpkin bread, but I've amped up the spices a bit and added a sugar-and-spice-studded lid atop the loaf. That seemingly small addition makes a big difference—while the bread bakes, the cinnamon sugar on top creates a tall, crisp lid, and it's everything we could ever ask for on a cool fall morning.

Yield: 8 SLICES

FOR THE BREAD

¾ cup (180 ml) vegetable oil

½ cup (105 g) granulated sugar

½ cup (120 g) packed brown sugar

¾ cup plus 2 tbsp (208 g) pumpkin puree (½ a standard 15-oz [425-g] can)

1 tsp vanilla extract

2 large eggs

1½ cups (210 g) all-purpose flour

½ tsp salt

1 tsp baking powder

1 tsp baking soda

½ tsp ground ginger

1¼ tsp (4 g) cinnamon

1¼ tsp (3 g) ground cardamom

¾ tsp nutmeg

½ tsp ground cloves

¼ tsp allspice

TOPPING (OPTIONAL)

¾ tsp cinnamon

1 tbsp (13 g) granulated sugar

½ tsp ground cardamom

PREP: Preheat the oven to 350°F (180°C). Line a loaf pan with parchment paper, and spray any exposed parts of the inside of the pan with nonstick spray.

MIX UP THE BREAD: In a large mixing bowl, whisk together the vegetable oil, granulated sugar and brown sugar. Add the pumpkin and whisk well. Add the vanilla and eggs and whisk until combined with the rest of the wet ingredients. Add the flour, salt, baking powder, baking soda, ginger, cinnamon, cardamom, nutmeg, cloves and allspice, and stir together until the last streaks of flour disappear, scraping the sides of the bowl as needed. Pour the batter into your prepared pan.

MAKE THE TOPPING (IF USING): In a dirtied dry-ingredient measuring cup, mix the cinnamon, sugar and cardamom. Sprinkle this over the top of the batter.

BAKE: Bake for 55 to 65 minutes. A skewer or knife inserted into the center of the bread should come out clean or with a few moist crumbs, not wet batter.

SERVE AND STORE: Let the bread cool in the pan as long as you can bear to wait before slicing it up. Slather on some butter and enjoy with a hot cup of coffee or tea. Store leftovers, once they've cooled, tightly covered, at room temperature for 3 to 4 days. This is best on the first day though, when it's still warm and the top of the bread loaf is crisp.

NUTELLA-SWIRLED *Banana Bread*

Since I grew up in a house where pumpkin bread was queen (Banana bread? Who's she?), I didn't really get to know banana bread until I was married, since it's my husband's favorite type of quick bread. He also loves Nutella, another treat that I was late to the party on. So naturally I had to combine the two into one perfectly moist, delicious loaf in honor of him. Now I'm a banana bread (and Nutella) believer!

Yield: 8 SLICES

⅓ cup (76 g) salted butter, softened at room temperature

1 cup (210 g) granulated sugar

2 large eggs

1¼ cups (200 g) mashed brown bananas (about 3–4 medium bananas)

⅓ cup (80 ml) water

1⅔ cups (234 g) all-purpose flour

1 tsp baking soda

¼ tsp baking powder

½ tsp salt

¾ cup (221 g) Nutella (name brand or off-brand both work)

PREP: Preheat the oven to 350°F (180°C). Line an 8½- or 9-inch (22- or 23-cm) loaf pan with parchment paper and spray with nonstick spray if the ends of the inside of the pan are exposed.

MIX UP THE BANANA BREAD: In a medium or large mixing bowl, cream the softened butter with an electric mixer. Add the sugar and mix until well combined. Add the eggs, mashed banana and water, and mix until just combined. Add the flour, baking soda, baking powder and salt, and mix just until the last bits of dry ingredients disappear into the batter, scraping the sides of the bowl as needed.

Pour half the batter into the prepared pan. Spoon half the Nutella over the batter. Use a butter knife to swirl the Nutella into the batter. Repeat with the remaining banana bread batter and Nutella.

BAKE: Bake for 60 to 70 minutes. The top will be a deep brown, and a skewer or knife inserted into the middle should come out clean or with a few moist crumbs. You don't want to see any wet batter.

SERVE AND STORE: Let the bread cool for as long as you can wait before digging in. Enjoy warm with a glass of milk. Let the bread cool completely before covering tightly. Leftovers are good at room temperature for 4 to 5 days.

Tip This recipe works well with gluten-free all-purpose flour.

GRANDPA'S SUNDAY SPECIAL
Coffee Cake

This is my Grandpa Gaub's recipe for coffee cake, but you don't just need to save it for Sundays. It's delicious any day of the week, with its thick, tall slices of fluffy cinnamon-flecked cake, a layer of juicy raspberry jam and a beautifully spiced crumb layer on top. Finish it off with a little drizzle of glaze, and resolve to only make this for all brunches forever.

Yield: 8-16 SLICES

FOR THE COFFEE CAKE

½ cup (1 stick or 113 g) salted butter, softened at room temperature

1½ cups (315 g) granulated sugar

2 large eggs

1 cup (240 ml) milk

2 tsp (10 ml) vanilla extract

3 cups (420 g) all-purpose flour

4 tsp (16 g) baking powder

¾ tsp salt

½ tsp cinnamon

¾ cup (240 g) raspberry preserves

FOR THE TOPPING

⅔ cup (160 g) packed brown sugar

¾ cup (105 g) all-purpose flour

2 tsp (6 g) cinnamon

¼ tsp salt

6 tbsp (85 g) cold salted butter

Infinitely Adaptable Glaze (page 157)

PREP: Preheat the oven to 350°F (180°C). Spray a 9-inch (23-cm) round cake pan with nonstick spray and line with parchment paper to allow you to lift the cake out for easy serving later.

MAKE THE COFFEE CAKE: In a large mixing bowl, cream the butter with an electric mixer. Add the sugar and mix until well creamed with the butter. Add the eggs, milk and vanilla, and mix until just combined. Add the flour, baking powder, salt and cinnamon, and mix, scraping the sides of the bowl as needed, just until the streaks of dry ingredients disappear into the batter.

Pour half the batter into the prepared pan—about 2¼ cups (540 ml) worth. Spread the raspberry preserves over the batter in an even layer. Pour the remaining cake batter and smooth it out. Scrape the bowl well. Give it a quick wipe with a kitchen towel if there are some batter bits you couldn't scrape up.

MAKE THE TOPPING: In the same bowl you mixed the batter in, whisk together the brown sugar, flour, cinnamon and salt. Cut the butter into roughly tablespoon-sized (14-g) cubes, and add them to the dry ingredients. Cut in the butter using a pastry cutter or clean hands, until you have pea-sized pieces and smaller. Sprinkle this evenly over the top of the coffee cake.

BAKE: Bake for 70 to 75 minutes. A skewer inserted into the cake should have some pretty moist crumbs but no wet batter. Let the coffee cake cool partially in the pan on a cooling rack, for about 20 to 30 minutes. Then, transfer to a rack and let cool for a while more before cutting. You can cut it once it's cool enough to handle, but still warm.

SERVE AND STORE: Drizzle with the Infinitely Adaptable Glaze (page 157), then slice and serve with coffee or milk. This makes 8 generous slices, or you can slice it into squares or thinner slices to yield 16 pieces. Store leftovers in an airtight container at room temperature for 3 to 4 days.

> *Tip* Make sure to use raspberry preserves and not a raspberry fruit spread—I find that the preserves have a better flavor.

MONKEY BREAD *Muffins*

I love monkey bread, but it's not the most practical dessert when there's no large crowd of people clamoring to be fed. Especially since this is one of those things that's best when it's hot from the oven—we don't want a pile of leftovers here. I've pared the recipe down into individual-sized muffins, and made the recipe small-batch. We're talking eight muffins, give or take a couple, made with a fluffy overnight brioche dough, plenty of cinnamon sugar and my quick 10-Minute Salted Caramel Sauce (page 150).

Yield: 8-10 MUFFINS

FOR THE DOUGH

3 tbsp (42 g) butter

½ tsp instant yeast

¼ tsp salt

2 tsp (8 g) cinnamon, divided

¼ tsp vanilla

1½ tbsp (23 ml) real maple syrup

¼ cup (60 ml) lukewarm water

1 large egg, at room temperature

1 cup plus 2 tbsp (158 g) all-purpose flour, plus more as needed

1 batch 10-Minute Salted Caramel Sauce (page 150)

2 tbsp (26 g) granulated sugar

Flaky sea salt (like Maldon brand), for topping (optional)

> *Tip* I usually mix up the dough at 8:00 or 9:00 p.m., move it to the fridge at 10:00 or 11:00 p.m. and then start assembling things at 8:00 or 9:00 the next morning. (I even let the dough go 1 hour extra in the fridge a few mornings, and they still turned out perfectly.)

MIX UP THE DOUGH THE NIGHT BEFORE: In a medium mixing bowl, melt the butter. Add the yeast, salt, ½ teaspoon of the cinnamon, vanilla, maple syrup, water and egg. Whisk together to combine, and then stir in the flour. The dough will be sticky and shaggy. Cover the bowl with a kitchen towel and let it rest for 2 hours on the counter. Then, cover the bowl tightly with plastic wrap or a lid, and refrigerate overnight (about 10 hours).

ASSEMBLE THE MUFFINS: The next morning, a bit before the chill time is up, line a muffin pan with muffin liners. Make the 10-Minute Salted Caramel Sauce (page 150) and add 1 tablespoon (15 ml) to the bottom of each liner. If you made it ahead and it was in the fridge, you'll need to microwave it for 30 seconds to 1 minute to loosen it back up.

Flour your counter well. Gently dump the dough out of the bowl, scraping any excess bits out. Sprinkle flour over the dough and flour your rolling pin. Gently press the dough down a bit. Roll the dough out to about 13 x 10 inches (33 x 25 cm). With a sharp knife, cut squares about 2 x 2 inches (5 x 5 cm). Roll each piece into a ball. You can piece together smaller end pieces to make a normal-sized ball. (This does not need to be perfect, but the balls should be about 1½ inches [4 cm] across.)

In the same bowl you used for the dough (give it a wipe with a kitchen towel first), mix together the remaining cinnamon and the sugar. Sprinkle a little cinnamon sugar in the bottom of each muffin cup, on top of the caramel sauce. Roll the balls in the bowl of cinnamon sugar, and add three of them to each muffin cup. Top each muffin with 1 teaspoon of caramel sauce and a pinch more cinnamon sugar. Cover with a clean kitchen towel and let rise for 30 minutes. Preheat the oven to 350°F (180°C).

BAKE: Bake for 18 minutes. The muffins will have risen and should be lightly browned.

SERVE AND STORE: Enjoy warm with an extra sprinkle of cinnamon sugar on top, more salted caramel sauce and even a pinch of sea salt if you like. These are best enjoyed fresh out of the oven. Leftovers can be stored in an airtight container in the fridge for 1 to 2 days. Gently reheat in the microwave.

RICH CHOCOLATE *Granola*

Anytime you can fit chocolate and breakfast into one recipe, I'm on board. The great thing about this recipe is that, while it tastes like a complete indulgence, it's actually relatively healthy—so don't yell at me for eating chocolate for breakfast, haha. The salty-sweet combo here is delightful, and so are those crisp, rich granola clusters. Get ready to fall in love. I know you will because the maple variation of this recipe is one of the most popular recipes on my blog!

 *Yield:* 6–8 SERVINGS

1½ cups (150 g) old-fashioned whole rolled oats

⅓ cup (32 g) shredded coconut (I prefer sweetened)

¼ cup (20 g) cocoa powder

⅛ tsp salt

¼ cup (52 g) raw turbinado sugar, divided

½ cup (58 g) roughly chopped pecans

⅓ cup (80 ml) olive oil

3 tbsp (45 ml) real maple syrup

1 tsp vanilla extract

½ cup (100 g) milk chocolate chips

Flaky sea salt (optional; I love Maldon brand)

PREP: Preheat the oven to 325°F (165°C). Line a large baking sheet with parchment paper.

MAKE THE GRANOLA: In a medium mixing bowl, stir together the oats, coconut, cocoa powder, salt, 2 tablespoons (26 g) of the turbinado sugar and pecans. Measure the olive oil into a 1-cup (240 ml) glass measuring cup, add the maple syrup and vanilla and whisk. Add this to the dry ingredients, and stir until everything is well combined.

BAKE: Spread the granola onto the prepared baking sheet in an even layer, and bake for 25 minutes, tossing the granola about halfway through to prevent over-browning around the edges.

Remove the baking sheet from the oven. Evenly sprinkle the chocolate chips over the granola, and return to the oven for 2 to 4 minutes, or until the chocolate is melty. Remove from the oven and sprinkle the remaining turbinado sugar and some flaky sea salt.

Let the granola stand at room temperature for 1 to 2 hours so it can cool and the granola clusters can set. If you don't care about having as many of those defined clusters, enjoy warm! Definitely let it cool, though, before putting it in a storage container.

SERVE AND STORE: Store leftover granola in an airtight container or glass mason jar at room temperature for up to 2 weeks.

> *Tip* To make this recipe gluten-free and vegan, be sure to use certified gluten-free oats and dairy-free chocolate. This granola makes a great gift! Gift it in a mason jar tied with a ribbon.

SAVORY *Bakes*

The baking world is certainly not limited to sweet treats, and this book is no exception! I wanted to include a handful of savory recipes for all your salty-tooth (is that a thing?) cravings. These recipes are simple, and I'm confident that any level of baker can pull these off. If you're not much of a yeast baker, don't worry—the two yeasted breads in here are simple enough for anyone to make.

I've got a savory bake for almost any scenario: Cheddar Cornbread Waffles (page 139) that can shapeshift into breakfast or dinner; Best Homemade Soft Pretzels (page 145) for a crisp, fall game day; crusty, No-Knead Cheddar and Thyme Bread (page 136) for cold-weather soup dipping; a Tomato Galette with Asiago and Gouda (page 143) that's bursting with late-summer flavor and color; and a Bacon, Cheddar and Gruyere Beer Bread (page 140) for an afternoon snack, any time of year. Oh, and the bread leftovers make incredible grilled cheese sandwiches. If, of course, you're lucky enough to have any slices left over.

NO-KNEAD CHEDDAR AND THYME *Bread*

No-knead bread is the lazy bread baker's dream. It's a stir-it-together, set-it-and-forget-it type of situation. You can let the dough hang out for 8 to 18 hours, and then it takes all of 30 seconds to shape it into a ball. Bake it in a Dutch oven for that perfectly crusty exterior, and prepare to dip this in any and all kinds of soups.

Yield: 8-10 SLICES

3 cups (420 g) all-purpose flour, plus more as needed

1½ tsp (9 g) salt

¼ tsp instant yeast

1¼ cups (115 g) shredded cheddar cheese

1 tbsp (3 g) chopped fresh thyme

¾ cup (180 ml) water, at room temperature

½ cup (120 ml) mild lager beer, at room temperature (I like Leinenkugel's Honey Weiss or New Glarus' Two Women)

MAKE THE DOUGH: In a large bowl, whisk together the flour, salt and yeast. Stir in the cheese and thyme. Add the water and beer, and stir until a dough forms. Make sure to stir in all the dry bits in the bottom of the bowl. Cover the bowl with a kitchen towel and let rest for 8 to 18 hours.

After the rest time is up, lay a big piece of parchment paper on your counter and dust it with flour. Gently dump the dough out onto the parchment paper. Gently fold the bread dough over onto itself for about 30 seconds to smooth it out and shape it into a ball. Let it sit on the counter, covered with a kitchen towel, for 1½ hours to rise. It should just about double in size.

BAKE: When you're ready to bake, get out a large Dutch oven. Make sure your oven rack is set at least halfway up in the oven to prevent the bottom crust from over-browning while baking. Score the top of the bread with a sharp knife in the shape of an "X." Using the parchment paper, lift the dough and lower it into the Dutch oven. (Your parchment paper should be large enough that the dough isn't going to be touching any exposed portions of the inside of the Dutch oven. Put the lid on the Dutch oven, place it into the oven, and then heat the oven to 450°F (230°C). Bake for 30 minutes covered, then remove the lid and bake for 25 to 30 minutes. A thermometer should register 200 to 205°F (93 to 96°C) when the bread is done, and the bread will be golden brown and sound crisp and hollow when you knock against the bottom of it with your knuckles.

SERVE AND STORE: Enjoy warm with plenty of butter and soup for dunking. Store leftovers in an airtight container at room temperature for 1 to 2 days or in the fridge for 3 to 4 days. Toast leftover slices or use for grilled cheese.

Tip You can use 1 teaspoon of dried thyme instead of 1 tablespoon (3 g) of fresh thyme.

CHEDDAR CORNBREAD *Waffles*

These waffles are a breeze to whip up! They're crisp around the edges and stuffed with cheese. Slather these with butter and maple syrup while they're piping hot, or top them with chili or pulled pork for a fun dinner.

Yield: **6 LARGE WAFFLES**

2 eggs, divided

¼ cup (½ stick or 57 g) salted butter

3 tbsp (45 ml) honey

2 cups (480 ml) milk

1¼ cups (175 g) all-purpose flour

1 cup (170 g) cornmeal

1½ tsp (9 g) salt

1¼ cups (115 g) shredded cheddar cheese

MAKE THE WAFFLE BATTER: Separate the egg yolks from the egg whites. (Keep the egg yolks in a spare measuring cup for later.) In a large mixing bowl, add the two egg whites and mix with an electric mixer on high speed until stiff peaks form. Scrape the beaten egg whites into a 1- or 2-cup (240- or 480-ml) glass measuring cup, and pop into the fridge until ready to use. Give the bowl a quick wipe. Melt the butter in the same bowl in the microwave. Whisk in the honey. Add the reserved egg yolks and milk and whisk well. Add the flour, cornmeal and salt and whisk until you can't see any streaks of the dry ingredients anymore. Stir in the cheese. Add the beaten egg whites directly from the fridge, and gently fold them in with a silicone spatula until you can't see any large white lumps, though a few white specks scattered throughout the batter is fine.

COOK THE WAFFLES: Heat your waffle maker over medium heat (mine goes from 1 to 5, and I used heat level 3). Spray with nonstick spray. Add ¾ cup (185 g) of the batter to the waffle iron, and cook for about 5 minutes. Your cook time will vary since every waffle maker can be a bit different, so keep an eye on the first one or two to get the hang of the cook time. The waffles will puff up and turn golden.

SERVE AND STORE: Serve hot with plenty of butter, maple syrup and bacon and eggs on the side. You can also serve these for dinner with pulled pork or chili. Store leftover waffles in an airtight container in the fridge for 3 to 4 days. Reheat in the microwave or in the toaster.

BACON, CHEDDAR AND GRUYERE *Beer Bread*

Beer bread is such a classic quick bread—and it's one of my favorite savory things to bake. I've amped up classic beer bread here by adding bacon, cheddar and gruyere cheese. And I've swapped honey in for granulated sugar to add even more flavor and to keep the bread nice and moist. Eat this while it's hot from the oven with plenty of butter. And, if you have any leftover slices, they make an INCREDIBLE grilled cheese.

Yield: 8–10 SLICES

3 cups (420 g) all-purpose flour

1 tbsp (12 g) baking powder

1 tsp salt

½ cup (57 g) gruyere

¾ cup (82 g) cheddar cheese

8 slices cooked bacon, cut into bite-sized pieces

1 (12-oz [355-ml]) bottle of pale lager beer (I used New Glarus' Totally Naked)

¼ cup (60 ml) honey

¼ cup (½ stick or 57 g) cold salted butter

PREP: Preheat the oven to 350°F (180°C). Line an 8½- or 9-inch (22- or 23-cm) loaf pan with parchment paper, and spray any exposed parts of the pan with nonstick spray.

MAKE THE BREAD: In a large mixing bowl, whisk together the flour, baking powder and salt. Stir in the gruyere, cheddar cheese and bacon pieces. Pour in the beer and honey, and stir until everything is well combined. Pour the batter into the prepared pan. Thinly slice the butter, and place the slices all over the top of the batter.

BAKE: Bake for 60 to 66 minutes. A knife inserted into the center should come out clean (I recommend this over a toothpick, so it can reach farther down). The top of the bread will be deep golden brown and crisp.

SERVE AND STORE: Let the loaf cool for about 20 minutes in the pan, and then lift it out using the edges of the parchment paper. Slice it and enjoy warm with plenty of salted butter and maybe even a drizzle of honey. Store leftovers in an airtight container at room temperature for 3 to 4 days, although this is best while it's warm from the oven.

Tip *I always cook my bacon in the oven on a foil-lined baking sheet for easier cleanup. I find it easier than dealing with stovetop oil splatter. Just follow the directions on the package for the bake time and temperature.*

Tomato Galette WITH ASIAGO AND GOUDA

This is the only thing I want to have for dinner all summer long—and even into the fall, while you can still get heirloom tomatoes. A blanket of colorful, juicy heirloom tomatoes lays atop a pile of asiago and gouda, and it's all nestled into a buttery, flaky pie crust. The directions for this recipe may seem a bit long, but I promise it's really a simple recipe. We're just making the crust, tossing together the tomato filling and then throwing it all together to bake!

Yield: 8 SLICES

FOR THE CRUST

¾ cup (105 g) all-purpose flour, plus more as needed

½ cup (70 g) white whole-wheat flour (You can sub for AP flour in a pinch)

¾ tsp salt

1 tsp granulated sugar

½ cup (1 stick or 113 g) cold salted butter

5 tbsp (75 ml) cold water, or more as needed

¼ cup (60 ml) cold full-fat sour cream

FOR THE FILLING

1½ lbs (680 g) heirloom tomatoes, sliced ¼" (6 mm) thick (about 5–6 medium tomatoes)

1 tsp salt

2 large cloves garlic, minced

Pinch of black pepper

¼ tsp garlic powder

¼ tsp dried basil

2 oz (60 g) gouda (about ⅔ cup)

2 oz (60 g) asiago (about ⅔ cup)

1 egg

MIX UP THE CRUST: In a medium mixing bowl, whisk together the all-purpose flour, whole-wheat flour, salt and sugar. Cut the butter into tablespoon-sized (14-g) cubes, and add them to the dry ingredients. Use a pastry cutter or clean hands to cut or rub the butter into the dry ingredients until you have chunks the size of walnut halves—some will be a bit bigger and some a bit smaller. Drizzle in the cold water and add the sour cream. Toss with a fork to mix in the water and sour cream.

Gently gather the dough into a ball. If the dough holds when you push it together, it's ready! If it's a bit dry and crumbles apart, add a bit more water, 1 tablespoon (15 ml) at a time, until it can hold a ball. You can also flick some water onto any dry bits hiding in the bottom of the bowl. Gently gather the dough into a ball and gently flatten it a bit into a 1-inch (2.5-cm) thick disk. Push any crumbly bits into place as best you can, and try to make sure there isn't a fissure in the disk that is causing it to fall apart. It may look a bit scrappy, but it should hold together. Wrap the disk tightly in plastic wrap.

Chill the dough in the freezer for 1 hour or in the fridge for at least 2 hours or up to 3 days. Once the crust has chilled for 1 hour in the freezer, move it to the fridge if you aren't quite ready to use it, so it doesn't freeze solid.

Preheat the oven to 400°F (200°C). Line a baking sheet with parchment paper or a silicone baking mat.

PREP THE FILLING: In a large mixing bowl, place the tomato slices, salt, garlic and pepper and set aside for 5 minutes.

(continued)

ASSEMBLE THE GALETTE: Flour your counter and rolling pin, and unwrap the dough disk. Sprinkle some flour on top of it, and begin rolling it out.

Start in the center of the disk, and gently roll the dough out in all directions. Turn the dough every few rolls to make sure it's not sticking to the counter. Lightly re-flour the counter if it is sticking, and sprinkle a little more flour on the dough. Smooth out/push together any cracked areas and continue rolling. Roll the dough out to about 14 x 14 inches (36 x 36 cm) and about ⅛ inch (3 mm) thick. (It doesn't have to be perfect!) Gently transfer the dough onto the prepared baking sheet by carefully rolling it up onto the rolling pin. If the edges are hanging over the sides of the pan, gently fold them in so they're lying on the dough.

Drain the liquid from the bowl of tomatoes, and then lay the tomatoes flat on a layer of paper towels. Blot them with two rounds of paper towels. Sprinkle the tomatoes with the garlic powder and dried basil.

Evenly sprinkle the cheese in the bottom of the rolled-out crust, leaving a 2- to 3-inch (5- to 8-cm) border around the edge. Place the tomato slices on top of the cheese in one layer, overlapping them a bit as needed and leaving behind any slices that don't fit. (They make a tasty snack!) Fold the border over the tomato slices, working in small sections at a time. Cover the galette with a kitchen towel, and chill in the fridge for 20 minutes.

BAKE: Beat the egg in a dirtied measuring cup with a fork, and brush this egg wash over the crust. Bake the galette for 45 to 50 minutes. The crust will be golden brown and should be crisp when you tap it. Don't be alarmed if you see some liquid on the pan around the galette—that's normal and it's never given my galette a soggy bottom.

SERVE AND STORE: Let the galette rest 5 to 10 minutes before slicing and serving. Enjoy immediately! This is best fresh, but leftovers can be stored in an airtight container in the fridge for 1 to 2 days.

Tip The prepared pie dough can also be stored in the freezer for up to 2 months. Move it to the fridge the day before you want to use it so it can thaw. I almost always make the crust a day ahead (just to break up the work) and chill it in the fridge overnight.

BEST HOMEMADE *Soft Pretzels*

There's something so perfect about biting into a fresh-baked pretzel, all covered in salt and melty butter. These are simple enough to make at home for a game-day snack, for Halloween or for a dunker with your favorite cold-weather soup. You can even replace the salt with cinnamon sugar!

Yield: **12 PRETZELS**

3 tbsp (42 g) salted butter, plus extra for optional topping

1½ cups (360 ml) warm milk

3¼ tsp (11 g) instant yeast

¼ cup (60 g) packed brown sugar

1½ tsp (9 g) salt

3¾ cups (525 g) all-purpose flour, plus more as needed

1 large egg

9 cups (2.1 L) water

½ cup (115 g) baking soda

Coarse sea salt, for topping

MAKE THE PRETZELS: Melt the butter in a large mixing bowl in the microwave. Measure the milk into a 2-cup (480-ml) glass measuring cup and warm it in the microwave for about 1 minute—it should be warm but not super hot. Pour the milk into the bowl with the butter, and add the yeast, brown sugar and salt, and whisk everything together. Stir in the flour.

Flour your counter well, and dump the dough onto it. Knead with floured hands for 3 minutes (set a timer). The dough will be smooth. Shape it into a ball. Spray the bowl (no need to clean it) with nonstick spray, and set the dough in the bowl. Cover with a clean kitchen towel and let it rise for 1 hour.

PREP FOR COOKING: Preheat the oven to 450°F (230°C). Line a few baking sheets with parchment paper or silicone baking mats. Beat the egg in a dirtied measuring cup for your egg wash. Add the water and baking soda to a large Dutch oven or pot. Whisk the baking soda into the water. Bring this to a boil while you shape the pretzels.

SHAPE THE PRETZELS: Dump the dough out of the bowl and gently press it down just a bit into an oval or rectangle about 9 inches (23 cm) across. Slice this into 12 equal wedges (each about 80 to 90 grams).

Working in batches of four pieces at a time, roll out each piece of dough with your hands, moving outward, until you have a rope 26 to 30 inches (66 to 76 cm) long. Pick up each end, twist them over each other and fold them down to form the pretzel shape.

Drop each pretzel into the baking soda bath (only add one or two at a time so they don't stick together) for 20 to 30 seconds. Don't let them go longer than this, or it will affect the taste. Remove them with a slotted flipper or a large serving spoon, letting the excess liquid drain back into the pot, and place the pretzels on a baking sheet.

(continued)

BAKE: Brush each pretzel with the egg wash and sprinkle with coarse salt. (If you're making these sweet, omit the salt.) Bake for 13 minutes. While this batch bakes, prep the next batch, and repeat until you've gone through all 12 pretzels.

SERVE AND STORE: Brush the pretzels with melted butter when they come out of the oven, and enjoy while warm. If using cinnamon sugar, dunk them in cinnamon sugar after brushing with melted butter. These are really best on the first day—I cannot stress that enough! You can store leftovers in an airtight container for 1 to 2 days, but really, eat them the first day, please.

FINISHING Touches

This chapter is dedicated to those little extra bits of a recipe that can take it right over the top. These elements can be used with so many recipes—even ones outside of this book.

We've got a decadent 10-Minute Salted Caramel Sauce (page 150) that's not sickeningly sweet like store-bought caramel can be. I'll show you how to make white chocolate and regular Chocolate Ganache (page 153) with a simple formula, and of course, you can adapt it to fit your taste by using semisweet, milk or dark chocolate. We've got the best Creamy Vanilla Frosting Base (page 154) that you can adapt for tons of recipes, and I share a simple trick that keeps my frosting from being tooth-achingly sweet.

There's also my three-ingredient Infinitely Adaptable Glaze (page 157) that can shapeshift into so many other glazes. Cherry! Key lime! Buttery maple! And more! And, I'll show you how to make the best homemade whipped cream (Classic Vanilla Whipped Cream on page 158). It's so simple, and I use a few tricks from my mom to keep it tasting so much better than the canned kind.

I hope you have fun exploring different pairings between the recipes in this book—and perhaps even recipes you already have in your repertoire—and these finishing touches.

10-MINUTE SALTED *Caramel Sauce*

This salted caramel sauce is an absolute dream. It requires just four basic ingredients and takes almost no time to whip up. It's silky and sweet, but not overly sweet like some store-bought caramel sauces can be. Drizzle this magic elixir over flaky hand pies, on top of ice cream, over gooey brownies or use it to flavor frostings.

Use the 10-Minute Salted Caramel Sauce in these recipes in this book: the Monkey Bread Muffins (page 131), the Salted Caramel Apple Galette (page 66), the Caramel Pear Hand Pies (page 75) or the Apple Snacking Cake with Oat Crumble (page 69).

Yield: **1¼ CUPS (300 ML)**

Note: I don't recommend doubling this recipe. Instead, make a few separate batches if you want more than one batch.

1 cup (210 g) granulated sugar

6 tbsp (85 g) salted butter, cut into tablespoon-sized chunks

½ cup plus 1 tbsp (135 ml) heavy cream

Pinch of flaky sea salt (I love Maldon brand)

Tip This makes a great gift! Tie a ribbon on the mason jar, and give it to someone as a housewarming gift, a thank you or a simple homemade holiday gift.

PREP: Set all your ingredients out before you begin so you're not digging around for anything while you have sugar cooking on the stove. If you have a metal whisk, keep a potholder handy, because the handle of the whisk will get very hot when you whisk in the heavy cream later.

MAKE THE CARAMEL SAUCE: Add the sugar to a medium saucepan (nonstick works great). Cook the sugar over medium heat, stirring constantly to avoid burning any of it. (I like using a wooden spoon here.) For the first few minutes, it will seem like nothing is happening, but eventually the sugar will begin to break down. After a few minutes, the sugar will start to become chunky, and then it will begin to melt into a coppery, caramel-colored liquid. Make sure all the little chunks of sugar are gone before you move on. If the sugar isn't completely liquified, the caramel sauce won't turn out, and it will seize up when you add the heavy cream.

Once the sugar has completely melted, with no small chunks remaining, reduce the heat slightly and immediately add the butter. Whisk constantly until the butter is completely melted. If the butter separates a little from the caramel, don't worry. Whisk it in as best you can, and continue to the next step. Remove the pan from the heat, and slowly stream in the heavy cream, whisking as you add it. The caramel will bubble up quite a bit here. If the caramel seems to harden in some spots, that's okay. It's just the cold cream solidifying some of the sugar. It'll melt back down in the next step.

Set the pot back on the heat for 1 minute, lazily stirring to let it thicken up a bit and melt any hardened bits. It'll be very bubbly. Remove the pot from the heat, and stir in the pinch of sea salt. Let it cool for at least 10 minutes before you use or store it.

SERVE AND STORE: Store the caramel sauce in an airtight container in the fridge for 2 to 3 weeks. (I keep mine in a glass mason jar.) When using it just out of the fridge, microwave it for 30 to 60 seconds to soften it back up.

Chocolate Ganache TWO WAYS

Chocolate ganache is the more sophisticated older sibling of melted chocolate. It keeps a beautiful shine, it only takes a few minutes to pull together and it tops so many desserts so beautifully. Drizzle it over brownies and cookies, decorate blondies and cookie bars with it and use it as the luscious top layer on a peanut butter tart.

Use these recipes with the Salted Chocolate Peanut Butter Tart (page 85), Funfetti Blondies with White Chocolate Ganache (page 52), Black Forest Cookies (page 16), Peppermint Mocha Cookies (page 27) and Apricot, Coconut and White Chocolate Oatmeal Cookie Bars (page 56).

Yield: **ENOUGH GANACHE TO DECORATE 1 BATCH OF COOKIES OR 2 BATCHES OF BAR COOKIES**

WHITE CHOCOLATE GANACHE

6 oz (170 g) good-quality white chocolate (use a baking bar like Ghirardelli or Baker's brand)

¼ cup (60 ml) heavy cream

Yield: **ENOUGH GANACHE TO DECORATE 1 BATCH OF COOKIES OR TO COVER THE TOP OF A 9-INCH (23-CM) TART**

CHOCOLATE GANACHE

8 oz (226 g) semisweet, milk or dark chocolate

1 cup (240 ml) heavy cream

The directions are the same for each type of ganache. Finely chop the chocolate. Add the chopped chocolate to a clean, dry bowl, making sure there's enough room to add the heavy cream on top.

Add the heavy cream to a small pot over medium heat and let it heat. Once it's at a simmer (bubbles starting to form around the edges, but not at a boil), remove from the heat. Pour the warm cream over the chocolate in the bowl, and let it sit for 5 minutes. Then, stir until it smooths out—you should have a smooth, creamy ganache.

If any of the chocolate pieces didn't melt, you can microwave the bowl of ganache for 8 seconds at a time, stirring in between, to get rid of any of those lumps. Be VERY careful with microwaving white chocolate as it can seize up easily, which is why you only want to let it go about 8 seconds at a time.

Use the ganache immediately—drizzle it over cookies or bars, or use it as directed in one of the recipes listed above. I don't recommend making the ganache ahead. It's best made right when you want to use it.

CREAMY VANILLA *Frosting Base*

This is truly the perfect vanilla frosting. No stovetop or complex methods required here—just your basics. The addition of my secret frosting weapon—cream cheese—keeps the frosting from being overly sweet. It's the perfect base to adapt to any recipe. I've mixed in salted caramel sauce, cocoa powder, raspberry preserves and even butterscotch pudding mix to flavor this frosting in a pile of ways.

Use this with the Malted Vanilla Birthday Cake with Chocolate Frosting (page 82), Raspberry Almond Cupcakes (page 65), Butterbeer Cupcakes (page 81) or any other dessert you love.

Yield: THIS RECIPE FROSTS A 9-INCH (23-CM) ROUND OR SQUARE CAKE LAYER OR EITHER OF THE CUPCAKE RECIPES IN THIS BOOK

¾ cup (1½ sticks or 170 g) salted butter, softened at room temperature

4 oz (113 g) cream cheese

3 cups (324 g) powdered sugar, divided

1 tbsp (15 ml) milk

1 tbsp (15 ml) vanilla extract

Pinch of salt

MAKE THE FROSTING: In a large mixing bowl, cream together the butter and cream cheese with an electric mixer on high speed until well creamed together. Add 1 cup (108 g) of the powdered sugar and the milk and mix until combined. Add the remaining powdered sugar, the vanilla and a pinch of salt, and mix until well combined. If the frosting is a bit too thick, mix in an extra splash of milk.

USE AND STORE: Spread or pipe the frosting onto any cake or cupcakes (or even brownies!) that you like. Make sure the dessert is completely cool before adding frosting or the frosting will melt right off. The frosting can be made a day ahead, covered tightly and kept in the fridge until ready to use. Before using, let it sit out a bit to soften back to a spreadable consistency.

INFINITELY ADAPTABLE *Glaze*

This glaze is truly infinitely adaptable. I've used it to frost homemade pop tarts, to top tart slice-and-bake cookies, to drizzle over warm cinnamon biscuits and to finish off snickerdoodle blondies. The base is a simple mixture of powdered sugar, milk and vanilla extract—and you can add almost anything to adapt it: cherry preserves, key lime juice, melted butter and maple syrup—you get the picture.

Use this on the Key Lime Slice-and-Bake Cookies with Key Lime Glaze (page 19), Zingy Homemade Cherry Pop Tarts (page 119), Maple Cinnamon Biscuits (page 108), Any Fruit Muffins (page 114), Caramelized White Chocolate Peach Scones (page 111), Small-Batch Gingerbread Scones (page 123), Grandpa's Sunday Special Coffee Cake (page 128) and more.

Yield: THIS RECIPE MAKES ENOUGH TO DRIZZLE OVER A COFFEE CAKE, A BATCH OF BAR COOKIES, MUFFINS OR BISCUITS OR ENOUGH TO DUNK A BATCH OF COOKIES IN

1¼ cups (135 g) powdered sugar

2 tbsp (30 ml) milk

½ tsp vanilla extract

In a medium mixing bowl, whisk together the sugar, milk and vanilla until nice and smooth. Use right away.

CLASSIC VANILLA *Whipped Cream*

Homemade whipped cream is so simple to whip up and so much better than the store-bought kind. It just takes a few basic ingredients, and you have a topping that's perfect for dolloping over slices of pumpkin pie or pineapple upside-down cake, for swooping onto berry cobblers and for topping a strawberry mojito pie.

Pair with No-Bake Strawberry Mojito Pie (page 86), Pumpkin Pie with Gingersnap Press-In Crust (page 72), Pineapple Upside-Down Crumb Cake (page 77) or any recipe in the Crisps, Cobblers and a Pandowdy chapter (page 89).

Yield: 2 CUPS (120 G) WHIPPED CREAM

1 cup (240 ml) cold heavy cream

2 tbsp (14 g) powdered sugar

1 tbsp (15 ml) vanilla extract

Make sure the heavy cream is very cold. In a medium mixing bowl, add the heavy cream, sugar and vanilla. Use a clean kitchen towel to cover the mixer and bowl, because this will splatter some. Beat with an electric mixer on high speed until stiff peaks form.

To check for stiff peaks, turn the mixer off and lift the beaters straight out of the bowl. If stiff peaks form and stand where you lifted the beaters out, it's done. Don't overmix the whipped cream or it will lose its smooth texture.

Don't make your whipped cream ahead of time—it's best when it's fresh.

Tips *Sometimes I stabilize my whipped cream, especially during the summer months or when it's quite humid. To do this, add ¼ teaspoon of unflavored powdered gelatin and 1 teaspoon of water to a small bowl. Swirl around so the gelatin is covered with the water. Let it sit for 5 minutes, and then microwave for 6 seconds, just to re-liquify it. Start mixing the heavy cream, and once it starts to thicken, but before it's done (about halfway through), slowly stream this into the bowl while you continue mixing. Continue mixing just until stiff peaks form.*

If serving with something like pumpkin pie or anything else that's fall-flavored, add a generous pinch of nutmeg along with the other ingredients. It's SO good!

ACKNOWLEDGMENTS

This book wouldn't be a reality without the support of my incredible husband, Grant. You've always encouraged me to go after my crazy dreams—first starting my blog, and then turning it into my full-time job, and now, making it through the wild process of writing a cookbook. I love you, and I'm sorry for shoving five different desserts in your face every day when you walked in the door from work. But after all, you are my #1 taste tester, ha!

Mom, I wouldn't love baking like I do if it wasn't for you and Grandma Kay! Thank you for putting up with my ulterior motives when I was younger (I was just in it for the raw cookie dough) and for answering my endless slew of texts and calls. Sometimes you tell me to "Google it," but we all know that moms are smarter than Google. And Dad, your jokes and attempts to name the book are always appreciated. Nathanael, your recipe testing over the summer was so helpful—thanks for putting up with me and my dad jokes (I blame Dad for those). I love you all.

Thank you to Haylie, my chief recipe tester—I wouldn't have made it through this process without your help. And thank you to Kodee, Kayla, Virginia, Kira and Abby for your recipe testing help. I truly appreciate you!

To my other taste testers—our neighbors, family members and Grant's coworkers—thank you for always being willing to consume ridiculous amounts of dessert and for your valuable feedback.

Last, but certainly not least, thank you to everyone who has visited my blog, read it, made my recipes and supported it over the years. I wouldn't have the opportunity to write a cookbook without your support. And thank you to Page Street Publishing for believing in me and my work. I will be forever grateful.

ABOUT THE AUTHOR

Stephanie is a mom-and-grandma-taught baker, and some of her earliest memories involve baking with her mom and grandmother. She started her blog, Blue Bowl Recipes, in August 2017, with the goal of sharing truly delicious recipes with people while giving them the confidence to make those recipes. She believes you don't need to spend all day fussing in the kitchen to bake a delicious cake, a perfect batch of cookies or a tray of fudgy brownies.

She began working on the blog as her full-time job in 2019, and continues sharing delicious recipes to this day. Stephanie spent time assisting in the test kitchens at Meredith for brands like Better Homes & Gardens, where she learned more about recipe development, testing and food styling, and has developed a few recipes for *Midwest Living* magazine.

She lives in Madison, Wisconsin, with her husband, Grant.

INDEX